We Defy!
A Tale Set in the Near Future

We Defy!
A Tale Set in the Near Future

by
Tommy L. Attaway, Jr.

To those who have gone this way before us.

Table of Contents

Preface

This is the time at which the author makes his usual disclaimer that all events depicted are fictional, and any resemblance to any person living or dead is entirely coincidental. Such precautions have been made in the creation of this work, with the establishment of characters and events merely to further the narrative of the story.

Of course such statements are widely discounted and rightly so. Obviously, I have come in contact with a number of personalities in life's journey, and elements of some of those personalities have contributed parts to various characters in this book. However, given the nature of the subject matter of this work, one may be tempted to take heed of Joseph Stalin when he is supposed to have said "Comrades, there are no coincidences."

This is another effort to contribute to a body of literature depicting the consequences of political and economic import to a people who have been badly served by those elected to office, appointed to government posts, and subjected to a legal system in which the rule of law no longer operates. The genre began with *Unintended Consequences* by John Ross, and later branched off with *Patriots!* into the realm of economic collapse as an addition to the type of literature with the "prepper" theme. This genre has now created an entire body of literature based on the themes of reaction to government misfeasance and economic calamity. Most of these works are by writers who have made their first literary efforts a warning of impending calamity.

With this story, I hope to add another perspective, along the lines of William Lind's *Victoria* (pen name Thomas Hobbes), which has as a conjecture, the break up of the United States due to substantial percentages of the population having conflicting cultural values. In that spirit, this work may be considered an exciting tale and just fun read. Or, the reader may consider it one more attempt to gaze into our future with a warning. And yet another reader, may find this to be a guide to conducting insurgency warfare in the western world. Such an exercise as to the purpose of this work is left to the reader to decide.

The title of this work, *We Defy!* should really be *Nous Defions!* This phrase has more meaning than only defiance, it also means to fight and to win as a result of that defiance. The phrase has a history within the US Special Forces community, and is part of the legend of the World War II OSS and its work with the French Resistance. The English title is used for ease of reference.

And lastly, my appreciation is extended to those who have supported and contributed to this effort.

Chapter 1

All the World is a Stage

In the mind of Jim Roberts there had been a long line of infringements and usurpations of the US Constitution that threatened the very foundation of the United States. That Constitution he swore to "preserve, protect, and defend" and even more, "to bear true faith and allegiance to the same" as an officer of the US Army. Many were the rationalizations put forth by others as to why this action or another was not the right time to "push back" and do something about it. One of the lessons Roberts learned in life is that it is a rare person who does not have a breaking point.

The breaking point for Jim Roberts occurred in 2005, with a case argued before the Supreme Court of the United States, Kelo v. City of New London. With this decision, it was now clear that no private property in the United States was safe from arbitrary seizure by any level of government. The United States in which Roberts believed was no more. There was no putting a happy face on it. The idea that anyone who could get himself elected or appointed to political office now constituted an ability to create a "compelling government interest" that could outweigh the rights and property of a citizen was preposterous on its face.

His post Army experience gave him several views into various facets of how the world worked. He saw US politics at close hand while working on a presidential campaign, the business world in a large company, and a look at the global financial system while at a major bank. Where some people saw various conspiracies, Roberts saw economics in action. Put a group of similar people together with incentives for certain behavior, it would hardly be surprising when that behavior is what happened. There was a natural tendency for people to acquire wealth and power, and once gained, few will willingly let it go. In his mind, the key to fairness was whether or not everybody got to play, or if it was a closed system that locked out undesirable people from competing with established interests.

Politics worked on the basis of what government can do for you or your business. The larger the government got, the more money there was to be bestowed on your allies, who had paid to get the office holder elected. It was all about steering money from government to your supporters. At the US federal level, this system was a gold mine as the Federal Reserve just printed all of the money Congress wanted to spend. There had to be a natural limit to that, especially once the debt got to the point where it would never be repaid. Either the credit card would get turned off, or there would be massive inflation. When that happened, the average people of the country would face massive taxation or their money would be worth nothing. Those who depended on money paid by the government would be wiped out financially. Those who actually owned things could survive, and those who could store wealth in hard assets would prosper.

This is where the political system and the banking system met. The trick was to obtain capital at minimal cost, and to buy an asset that either generated income, or would appreciate in value. Traditionally, the mechanism to do this had been the stock market. Investors such as Warren Buffett, had amassed tremendous wealth by carefully selecting the stock of companies destined to grow by being in the right business at the right time. The financial services industry still operated on the idea that almost anyone could do this if they just invested in the correct mutual funds. Roberts had concentrated in money and capital markets in MBA School. This method of wealth creation only worked with a growing economy and efficient markets.

The free market was heavily distorted by government regulation, tax policy, and Federal Reserve fiscal policy. In Roberts view, no sane individual would be invested in the stock market. The financial institutions had every advantage, borrowing from the Fed at rates even below .5% interest, executing trades at no cost to themselves, and raking in the placement fees on deals relating to initial offerings, mergers, and acquisitions. Even the wealthy investor who played this game was along for the ride. The only way for the individual to win, was to be the majority owner of a company that one of the capital management firms wanted to buy.

The financial services industry spent millions of dollars on political campaigns, because the industry made billions in profit based on the government tax code determining what was a capital gain, a loss, tax deductible expenses, and so forth. Both major political parties played this game, one was happy just to rake in the cash, the other demanded a symbolic tribute from the industry in terms of low income home loans, and other programs for its supporters written into law. As long as the tax loss write off was there, nobody in the financial services industry complained. Everybody involved went away happy, and the country went further in debt.

One party bought votes with entitlement payments, and the other was successful in fooling the taxpayers into thinking that they would control government while buying government goods and services from campaign contributors. Both were only interested in raiding the public treasury. One thing was clear for individuals – the day of a long term career to retirement working for the same company for an entire career in the private sector was over. The easiest way for an individual to lead a middle class lifestyle was as a government employee. The wealthiest communities in the country were clustered around Washington, DC and the state capitals.

The income tax system worked to prevent social mobility. A wealthy person with one million dollars could put that money in tax free municipal bonds and make $50,000 per year tax free. If an employee made $50,000 per year, at least one third of that sum went away via various taxes. Capital accumulation was being prevented by progressive income tax rates, and it was not much of a challenge to get most people to vote to support even more of that tax policy and make themselves poorer in the process.

The confluence of the failure of the public schools, and a government that rewarded not working, ensured a labor force that was generally non competitive in a world wide economy. A country with an economy based on making things tended to correlate to a growing economy, and an increase in standard of living. Such were the dictates of economics.

Thus the question, of how is it possible for the individual to achieve economic success under these circumstances. Roberts pondered this question, not only for personal reasons, but for the good of the country as well. A prosperous population does not riot and overthrow governments. Widespread discontent leads to political instability. The situation is made even worse, when there are organizations promoting instability for their own purposes. What was clear was that the country was not getting better, and the quality of life was getting worse for the majority of Americans.

On top of all of this was the conflict of cultures which placed western civilization in peril. Throughout history, religion has been a powerful motivator. Western civilization was being attacked on both flanks. On one flank was the expansion of Islam, which is intent on conquering the world and placing all populations under its control. On the other flank was the religion of secularism, masking its motives under the guise of science and reason. Or, as Roberts though of it, the religion of anti God. He was a product of the Cold War, and Roberts had seen the communist methodology used to attack the west. It was in almost all respects the same tactics used by the secularists, who had taken the long march through the institutions of the society in order to mount their attack on western civilization.

What had happened in the Untied States was only a symptom of a wider conflict, which was the question of the survival of western culture. Roberts saw three threats to western civilization, two external, and one internal.

The external threats were the easier to see, and to defend against because they could be seen. Successful defense was primarily a matter of will. Russia and the Peoples' Republic of China were in many ways traditional national competitive threats. With the exception of being a nuclear power, Russia was primarily a regional threat to peace in Europe, but had a long history of military equipment diplomacy, and thus fomenting regional conflict via insurgency movements against western countries. The largest threat Russia posed to the US was that type of support in the past, and possibly the present, of movements internal to the US that tended to place Marxist sympathizers into positions of influence on public thought.

The PRC was more of an expansionist threat. In power for over 60 years, the Communist Party of China had created a world power and were intent on using that power. There was no doubt that they intended to dominate Asia, and this would threaten the independence of countries that had become more western in outlook toward individual liberty. Most of these countries were also US allies – Republic of China (Taiwan), Republic of Korea, Japan, and the Philippines.

Most dangerous was the long term and deliberate planting of agents of influence throughout the United States. By the end of the 20th Century, most westerners would say that Communism was dead and the capitalist west had won the Cold War. While this was true in the sense of a military confrontation, the political ideology of Marxism lived on. Originally, Marxism was based on economics. As one writer noted, Communism failed because people like to own things. For a committed communist, any failure is only a temporary setback on the longer road to victory.

Thus, Communists studied why their plans did not succeed in the 20th Century. They decided the key was still the problem of the middle class. The existence of the capitalist middle class has always presented a challenge to the success of international Communism. Even Marx had found the middle class problematic. They always aligned with the capitalists, rather than the masses from which they originated. That such class traitors needed to be eliminated along with the capitalist class was unquestioned. But as long as the middle class existed, their numbers would stand in the way of the enlightened class of communists establishing the dictatorship of the proletariat.

Communists had expected success early in the 20th Century with World War I. The masses would realize that the capitalists would sacrifice them for money and power by profiting from the war. However, the vast majority of the people patriotically answered the call of duty from their countries, went into the trenches and died. Only in Russia, were communists able to achieve success with the aid of a largely uneducated population recently freed from serfdom. Once a power base was established, the remaining intellectuals in the government and church were liquidated in less than two years. Then the serious work of creating the modern man could begin

The action now shifted to political struggle to set the stage for armed revolution. The 1930s saw this strategy come close to success in the west, but only made post World War II advances in poor, unindustrialized countries. It was clear to the dedicated communists that the western middle class and the society which forms it, had to be destroyed in order to achieve power. Therefore, the foundations of western society had to be targeted for attack. A working group was put together to study this problem.

In an economic sense, what makes the western middle class possible is education. This facilitates invention, which allows for the productivity gain which the storage and application of knowledge can foster. This stimulates economic activity, which produces goods for people to own and improve their lives. This economic activity depends on a society that respects property rights and the value of an individual who can exercise those rights. And the very idea of an individual with worth as an individual is based on religion – specifically the Jewish and Christian religions. That religious foundation provided the foundation for families, another foundation of western thought which bound people together that would interfere with Marxist goals.

Therefore, the objects of attack became clear to committed Marxists. To eliminate the western middle class, the religion, educational attainment, and legal protections of individuals had to be destroyed. Once the values that upheld the culture were gone, the middle class would gradually disappear, and the resulting impoverished masses would then be ripe for the revolution to be led by the enlightened intelligentsia, who would then create the modern man and eliminate the undesirable elements standing in the way of progress.

The first point of attack is to create Party Organs which would work to indoctrinate the masses with the party line. The organs would coordinate the propaganda activities to replace information sources that were not aligned with the party. Over time, more of the people would have their ideas and perceptions of truth created via one or more of the Party Organs acting in concert. To control information is the means to start to control thought.

This led to the second point of attack. The western education system was now state run, and therefore capable of being subverted to the use of the party. This gave Marxists access to the education of youth, future teacher selection and placement, journalists, and future government officials, who would have to be sanctioned by the universities in order to be able to engage in their professions. Control of the education of the young is the fastest way to change a society. In time, only permitted opinions could be voiced, or the credentials needed for certain occupations could be withheld.

Government was ripe for exploitation. It is the tendency of government officials to want to accumulate power, so it is only necessary to put your people in government in order to have that power put to your use. In each of these areas it was possible to obtain the services of any number of useful idiots who would not even be aware that they were acting a part in which they had no idea of the intended end, and even if they did know, would probably not object to that end as long as they maintained their personal power.

Religion was the most difficult to attack. Thousands of years of heritage are not discarded overnight. This also required a multi level attack. One method of attack was to attack faith with the criticism of religion based on science and appeal to reason. Thus, the very idea of faith is held to public ridicule, with reinforcement in the minds of children via the science taught in schools, and the adults are attacked via the legal system for faith based actions. Finally, the personal restraint taught by religion is attacked via an appeal to two very powerful human emotions – sex and power.

The temptation was too great for many westerners to resist. Many went the route of Faust, and became uneducated, immoral, hypersexual narcissists. If a family resisted, the children would be removed from the parents for the protection of the children by agents of the state. For the truly proficient practitioners, there could even be a starring role on television. Western civilization was committing suicide, and doing so eagerly.

As a university student, Roberts had studied Marx, and as a military officer, studied communism and Leninism in order to know how his opponents thought and how they operated. There was no doubt in his mind about all of this being a coincidence with no design behind it.

One thing was for certain. It was much more fun to fight communists overseas with a number of your fellow soldiers.

Fighting communists in your own backyard without any help was not going to be enjoyable at all.

As an individual, one could only try to limit the negative impacts of all of this upon you. Efforts made by individuals to fight these trends were generally ineffective. It takes the synergy of organized activity to turn the tide.

In one sense the "prepper" movement was a reaction to all of this. The idea, that one could buy and build a retreat where all of this impending doom could pass you by was emotionally appealing. Roberts thought that was an unrealistic approach in that there was no place to hide from a dominant culture bent on total control. It was not possible to avoid a fight that targeted you.

Chapter 2

Sent Hither a Multitude of Officers

By 2015, it had become next to impossible to operate a small business in the United States of America. Every level of government and any number of semi public entities may have a veto over the use of your property, capital, and even labor. There were uncountable laws and regulations to which every person and business was subject. It was impossible to know and comply with every edict promulgated by an unknown number of political and semi political jurisdictions. At any time, an enforcement action could be brought against the business. The owner could be certain that the cost of defense against such edicts would be financially, if not emotionally ruinous.

It started with your birth certificate, because without one, it was impossible to prove being a person to the relevant authorities. This certificate allowed one to enroll in school, later obtain a driver's license, a passport, or any other document society might require of you. More importantly, it was necessary to obtain a social security number. Without such a number, you were not a dependent on your parents' tax return (assuming a child was a member of a family with more than one parent), or could be employed, or join the military, and of even greater consequence, open a bank account, obtain credit, or any other number of activities constituting a part of modern life.

Somehow, the founders of the United States had fought a revolution, founded a country, and set the foundations for personal liberty in place without needing any of that. Roberts was certain that the people of the 18th Century had figured out how to have children and conduct commerce without the benefit of government institutions dedicated to keeping track of people.

And then your child could be subjected to the public school system. This is where the cultural indoctrination by forces hostile to western civilization began. The real purpose of the federal Department of Education was to impose control of the content taught in public schools. This control made it possible to put into place a cultural norm that was determined by those groups interested in creating the type of people suitable to their purposes. This scheme had an over 100 year history, starting with the education theories of John Dewey, who thought the public schools could produce people trained to be cooperative workers for trades and factories, while being good citizens obedient to their government.

In the early 1900s, teachers were hired predominately from a pool of educated single women, as teaching being an occupation acceptable to society for unmarried women. Dewey and other intellectuals promulgated their theories of education to university personnel in the progressive movement, who saw the potential in making people into the mold they had in mind for society. Part of controlling education is controlling the credentials required for people who can work in that occupation. This lead to certificates being required to be a public school teacher, and later to have any of the senior administrative jobs. Of course, the education profession would establish what constituted proper certification. No longer could school boards hire such local people they wanted to teach their children, they now had to hire qualified professional teachers, or lose their government funds.

Thus, the state education boards, and finally, the federal Department of Education was created in order to monitor the public schools for compliance to government rules and the money provided for school programs. Eventually, less than half the employees of a school system were primarily tasked with teaching children. The US school system became the first stage in indoctrination of acceptable thoughts and behaviors, in the manner of Nazi Germany, or the Soviet Union. The products of such a system were largely uneducated in western civilization, science, and reasoning ability. The more extensive the credentials, the less meaning those credentials had.

An uneducated population is at a disadvantage in a highly competitive world. Businesses faced the expense of training a workforce that had few real skills. Sound management decisions require people with cultural awareness and sound judgment. The universities produced graduates highly judgmental with a limited awareness of the cultural history of western society and an inability to manage or influence other people by use of reason.

Government had become the largest growth industry in the United States. One in five people employed in the US economy were government workers or contractors. And given the way many grant programs worked, that number was probably low. There were some interesting demographics in government employment. Women outnumbered men two to one in public sector employment, and almost 50% of all blacks with university degrees had government jobs.

The demographics of government employment raised a chicken and egg question. Were the demographics the result of government policies, or did the people hired lead to the policies? Roberts figured the policy came first – you hire people to carry out the policy you want. And that was certainly what Roberts was going to do if he could find enough people to carry out a plan that was forming in his mind.

After all, look at the impact of the people who were selected to become federal judges. They had become a de facto elite who considered themselves superior to the mere citizenry subject to their jurisdiction, and paid only token obedience to the political class that had placed them in power. The trend had been set in motion in 1833 with the publication of Supreme Court Justice Joseph Story's work on the Constitution. He considered the judges to be the proper repository of the final decision making of rights and the Constitution. This was because the judges, as beings devoted to the law and reason, were not subject to the whims of popular opinion and changing attitudes. It was also the beginning of the end to the idea that the Constitution was creation of the States, and thus the federal government was a child of the States, and subject to the consensus of the States. Instead, the idea took hold that the federal government was a creation of the people and to be superior to the States in every respect.

We were now living with the consequences of that view of government. The law was no longer the text of the Constitution or statute, the law was the opinion of a superior court. When there was no prevailing court opinion, the law was what the judge said it was. In order to lead their lives, people need a degree of predictability, essentially the ability to know what is legal and what is not before the fact. For courts to decide the legality of an act without any predictability, meant that for most people there was no law, because they could not reliably know in advance if an act was legal or not.

At the core of the problem was the fact that the US Congress, and by extension the rest of the federal government no longer recognized any limits to its authority. It passed laws unimpeded by the US Constitution, essentially saying we give authority to agency X to make up any regulation it thinks necessary. Agency X always found it necessary to make regulations. Complain as they may to their Congressional representatives about this, nothing changed. It was always the people in Washington who could not be persuaded to do things differently claimed the Representatives, the votes to stop them just were not there. Never mind that any number of Congressmen campaigned on stopping that activity. Every federal agency had benefactors that contributed money to Congressional campaigns. And the cancer spread.

Thus, people and business were subject to thousands of pages of regulations, each with the force of law, never voted on by a legislative body, and enforced by numerous agents of government, armed and able to arrest any citizen at any time, for any violation. The United States now had more in common with the Soviet Union of 1930 to 1990, than it did with the country founded in 1776.

The perfect example of how far wrong it had gone, was the concept of an administrative law judge. The agency that created a rule to which a citizen was subject, created its own legal process with a lawyer selected by the agency, which would be the judge of whether a citizen accused of a violation was guilty or not. Even the Soviet Union had kept the pretense of having a functioning impartial court system with a prosecutor.

The number of entities at the federal level was bad enough, but the same thought patterns that produced the federal Leviathan, also operated at the state level. Just the scope and field of endeavor changed. Property owned by individuals was frequently the target of state government, along with professional qualifications. There was hardly any property that could escape taxation, the County Appraisal Board having the power to determine the value of your possessions and land, which then became subject to tax. The lesson of Shay's Rebellion, of what happened when people with no money were taxed on their property, had been forgotten. The serfs now rented their land and property from the state instead of the local nobleman.

The auto insurance industry was a perfect example of how an industry got a state legislature to pass laws and regulations to its benefit, while portraying to the citizens that the state was keeping the industry under control. First, a law is passed requiring the driver to have some form of auto insurance or post a bond. In exchange, a state regulatory board is created to set insurance rates. The insurance industry is exempt from anti competition laws other business must follow in exchange for regulation. If you want to get in on the deal and start you own insurance company because of the profits made by the others, you have to meet the qualifications of the state regulatory authority in order to get permission to do business.

Then if a citizen had to deal with an insurance company in any capacity other than paying money to it, more regulations kicked in. If your car was damaged by someone, you couldn't just negotiate a payment for your inconvenience. The repair work was paid to the shop making the repairs in order to prevent individuals from just pocketing the money for the damage done to them. Unless the insurance company would rather just pay what it considered the market value of your car, and take it from you. The legal principle that an injured party was entitled to have his property put back into the state it was before damage to the extent possible, and a money value placed on what could not be repaired was gone. That would make it too expensive to have accidents and damage other people's cars. Of course, Roberts thought that was the point of the law, otherwise there would be a penalty for not being responsible for what one did.

Certain occupations required permission from the state in order to be employed in such work. Favorite targets for paying to be "trained" and meet requirements, included but was not limited to, air conditioner repair, barbers, hairstylists, florists, security guards, and so on. The medieval guild system was alive and well. The system required you to pay to play. Or, to put it in terms an economist would use, there were artificial barriers to entry into the market that in effect reduced competition. This harms the economy by keeping prices to consumers artificially high in order to protect the existing suppliers of goods and services.

Towns and cities got in on the act with zoning boards, permits for garage sales, and ticketing kids for selling lemonade without a business license or certificate of health inspection. There was an inspector to check the height of your grass, at your expense, of course. Food service inspections were another revenue generator. If not for the beneficial power of government, food outlets would poison their customers so that the customers would never eat at that food outlet again.

It was the considered assessment of Jim Roberts that freedom was moving backward, not forward, and as a people, we were less free than the founders of the United States intended. He was certain that there were many others who shared his observations and conclusions. And he was also certain that the men who had bequeathed this heritage to him would expect Jim Roberts to do something about it. The founders were men of the Age of Reason, and had done their best to set in motion a scheme of ordered liberty.

Roberts understood why the current situation evolved and was not corrected because he had read Solzhenitsyn. When some small infringement of liberty occurred, it would be too much trouble to take the time and effort to redress every minor affront. And just like every little occurrence that led to arrest and being sent to a Soviet Gulag, every infringement of liberty ultimately led to tyranny. Every one of those rules seemed to have good reasons behind it. It would be unreasonable to do away with these inconveniences, when they produced so much good for society. The road to Hell had been paved with good intentions, but the destination was Hell, just the same. The only way to maintain freedom was the disproportionate overwhelming response to any threat to liberty as soon as it was detected. That was the lesson of history.

In summary, every government agency or board was the result of some constituency or organization wanting the government to use its power on their behalf. If elections really meant anything, changing who was in power would lead to the elimination of the agencies supported by the losing side. This would lead to wide swings in the focus of government activity, and make political campaigns high risk activities. When there got to be enough money involved, it was no longer required to close down the agencies supported by your opponents, and your opponents would not shut down your agencies. A reasonable accommodation had been made that everyone could live with, that would lower the stress of political campaigning.

18

The problem with groups like the Tea Party is that they did not want government to do something for them, and that made it hard for the political class to relate to such people. The Tea Party wanted something different, they wanted to take away other peoples' benefits and obtain no benefit other than more freedom for everyone. Modern politics didn't work that way. Reasonable people were willing to compromise to give something to the other side, this is the way good government worked. Office holders got elected to do things for people, not to reduce the scope of government and reduce the number and amount of government contracts and entitlements.

However, Jim Roberts was an unreasonable man, and he was seeking other unreasonable men.

He was reminded of the Norwegian resistance fighter of World War II who said, "My country has been stolen from me sir, and I want it back."

Jim Roberts was a man on a mission.

Thomas Jefferson had figured out how to run a national government that functioned without individuals having to pay a tax to it. That was how it was supposed to work. It could be made to work again.

Chapter 3

A Well Regulated Militia

Having reached the conclusion that economic and government collapse was going to be inevitable, there were two options. Wait for it to happen and then deal with it. Or, take mitigating actions now. Roberts chose the latter. Given the consequences that would occur with the collapse, Roberts decided to check out the militia movement as a probable avenue to find people who would understand what it would take to make it through the worm hole the country was likely to traverse and come out on the other end alive. There were any number of militia websites and message boards out there. The trick would be to navigate through all of that to find a group that were like minded and had a clue about what to do, with out sticking out too much and becoming a target of interest to an overbearing government themselves.

The citizen militia movement got its modern start in the early 1990s as a result of the actions by the ATF on raids that resulted in the deaths of agents and citizens who had violated no firearms laws, or had obviously been entrapped into a technical violation. The result was that some gun rights advocates dusted off the history of the Second Amendment and old militia laws, using them as a basis to form groups armed for common defense. This activity ultimately caused a legal dilemma. The authorities adamantly believe that the only valid militias are those organized by a government. The militias pointed to research that indicated the people have formed militias themselves in keeping with the right of freedom of association. Some of those arguments on both sides were self serving. The militias tended to overlook the requirement that private militias have the same obligations as state organized militias. The government conveniently overlooked the historical record of privately organized militias being accepted into service as a unit in the Army of the United States as late as the war with Spain.

By inclination and training, Roberts aligned with the regulars in the standing army. In many ways he was still a soldier, even if the Army no longer had any use for him. The founders were clear in their intentions via the adoption of the Constitution, the Second Amendment, and the Militia Act of 1792. The militias of the several states were to be the repository of military power and the building blocks of a national army when one was needed. As with the other regular officers, he agreed that this was a very inefficient military system, as the quality of officers he had seen in reserve component units was all over the place, and that made mobilizations difficult.

However, the oath taken to the Constitution meant that was the system the Army was bound to support. The whole concept of the National Guard had turned the military system envisioned by the founders on its head. The National Guard system was exactly what the Anti – Federalists had warned against and why the Second Amendment existed. The last and ultimate repository of military power in the United States was supposed to be in the people themselves.

It took a few months, but some careful networking found a couple of other former soldiers with the same view of the world. They decided to visit a militia exercise being held elsewhere in the state, and got themselves invited to attend.

All experience is useful, even a bad experience as long as something is learned in the process. Of course, that assumes you don't get killed in the process of learning. It was a disappointing experience to see what passed for a militia in action. They were lacking combat arms vets as the trainers, so it was a case of the blind leading the blind. That would have to be fixed, if these militia units were going to be able to do anything useful.

 The decision by Roberts and the other vets to start their own unit was an easy one. The Militia Act of 1792 would be the model. They decided not to advertise that they were building a new unit. That would tend to perpetuate existing problems. Any number of people would jump in for any number of different reasons, few of which would be good. That would be very tempting for a sting operation by a government agency or for some wannabe colonel who would try to push everybody else out of the way to try to gain command.

The smart play was to create a unit that appeared to already exist, with that message sent via a unit website. This would attract people who were interested in joining a unit and more willing to take assignments that would lead to building a functioning military organization. A domain name and web site were easy enough to acquire and build, thus in less than a week, Texas had another private militia within its borders.

Roberts took his experience with the National Guard as the training model. They would take the one weekend a month without the two weeks in the summer as the training time that would be available. Next step was to create an organizational structure and training plan around the parameters of time and equipment that was likely to be able to be procured.

As an organizational structure, Roberts chose the light infantry company of the US Army. It was an organizational structure that many vets would be comfortable with. Such a company was light on unit equipment, thus it would be easier to replicate what such a unit would have within it. The training manuals produced by the Army would more closely match the people, equipment, and structure for integration into a training plan. The unit would start small and grow itself into a company someday, if there was success.

The training plan was also modeled on how the National Guard did unit training. They would do indoor training during the cold months, because the new guys especially, would be lacking gear for operating in cold weather. It was more important to get in the training than it was to be able to operate in cold weather. Texas would supply enough cold weather later. Early in the training year, focus on individual military skills, ending with rifle qualification, move on to team training, and finally the ability to operate as a unit.

In devising the training plan another Army concept was used, the Unit Mission Essential Task List (METL). Mission was the first consideration because all training depended on the missions that the unit would be expected to perform. This is the first major decision a commander makes, because the time and resources required to train everything are seldom there. Roberts chose the following company level missions (A) Conduct Stability Operations (B) Conduct Security Operations (C) Conduct Defensive Operations (D) Provide Sustainment.

Each Mission was further refined into group tasks Roberts thought the unit would have to be able to perform. From the Stability list, he chose Conduct Civil Security, discarding Conduct Civil Control from the list as he expected to operate in an area where his unit would not be the effective civil government – that would already exist. From Security Operations he chose Provide a Screen and Conduct Operational Area Security, and decided that Conduct Guard Operations didn't make the cut. Conduct an Area Defense was added to the company group task list, and Conduct Logistic Support rounded out the company list. The platoon list would be longer as the collective task list was matched to the mission. The whole matrix took about 125 pages in an Army manual.

While that was the big picture, most of the militia members would have individual and team tasks that supported the unit tasks. Thus, while an individual was training on task 071-326-0501 Move as a Member of a Fire Team, his team leader was performing task 071-326-5805 Control Movement of a Fire Team, which was part of a collective task 071-450-0041 Conduct a Point Ambush, which was a part of Conduct Defensive Operations. The advantage to the Army having thousands of people in Training and Doctrine Command writing military manuals, was that Roberts could devise a plan of what the militia would need to know, and who in the militia would need to know what, without having to figure it out for himself and maybe forget something important on that list.

The training plan was then fit into the monthly weekend training for the year. This was unlike what Roberts saw many other militias doing, and in his mind, why those other militias were minimally effective. They tended to do the same thing weekend after weekend. Part of that was understandable in terms of the constant personnel turbulence (lose and gain new people every month), but the leaders had limited experience in running a unit and only the prior service combat arms guys would have even seen a military unit in operation. So few of the militia leaders had an idea about how limited their experience was, and that was limiting unit capability. Roberts decided to live with the other problem of people always "coming in during the middle of the movie" as they would not have pervious training needed in order to do the current training well. The NCOs and time would catch them up as fast as possible. It was just the nature of the beast.

Unit standards and how strictly they would be enforced would be the next issue to confront Roberts. He had selected the woodland BDU / desert DCU combination as the uniform and equipment pattern. This was done for several reasons. The pattern had all field gear needed made in that pattern. It was plentiful, as the Army had used it from 1981 to 2005, and this tended to make it cheaper than other patterns available. It had an additional advantage of having been widely recognized by the citizenry as their military – this concept might prove important later. Widespread availability made it possible to do some bulk buying and make it available to the members at less cost than the alternatives. This would help make the standard self enforcing by making going against standard more expensive to the members than staying within the unit standards.

Weapons would be another sticking point with the typical militia. There was the tendency to make a virtue of necessity. Too many people on tight budgets tried to convince themselves and others, that bolt action rifles which were already obsolete when World War II started, still had a place for the average soldier in modern conflict. Except for very specialized tasks, semi automatic weapons were a requirement for the modern battlefield. Roberts went with the NATO approach, in that the AR was preferred, but either 5.56mm or 7.62mm NATO ammunition use was required. No exceptions were allowed, weapons had to match the ammunition types that would be stockpiled, so a common supply was possible. Anyway, a quality AR could be built for a reasonable price. The vets would see the logic of this and help convince the others.

This was a modern example of how what Roberts was doing aligned with the Militia Act of 1792. Every citizen was required to be part of the militia, equipping himself at his own expense with a military grade weapon of a standard caliber, field equipment, a basic load of ammunition, and a uniform of the style chosen by the brigade commander.

In another instance of the US Constitution being turned on its head, the gun hating federal government had pointed to the Militia Act of 1792 as authority for mandating the purchase of health care. This had made the perversity complete.

Chapter 4

A Tireless Minority

One of the members of the militia that Roberts led was a fan of an internet radio station called Rampaging Elephants, which evidenced their support of Tea Party Republicans. The morning host was sponsoring a meeting of as many Texas militia leaders as he could get to attend. Roberts got himself invited to the meeting. He was interested in coordinating activities with any other groups that could be found that had some ability to function as real units.

Most similar efforts had been total failures. They turned into little more than rugby scrums, with various commanders trying to position themselves as the commander of all of the militias in the state. Such an attitude demonstrated several bad qualities. It represented the typical top down thinking of most militia units. They appointed any number of officers, and then might or might not make an attempt to recruit people to fill in the hollow units they created. Or they would try to get the independent units to take a place in their organizations by what Roberts called mutual recognition – if you recognize me as colonel of the Texas militia, I'll recognize you as the captain of our unit for your region.

Thus, Texas had ended up with three to five state wide "Texas" militias, and some number of units that operated independently of any other militia organization. If the units would cooperate with each other, progress could be made in terms of sharing information and mutual aid. That would be the basis for some form of area defense, or deterrence if nothing else. But, these people had to be willing to talk to each other.

The most important reason why Roberts wanted to attend was to meet the Rampaging Elephants host. Those guys were in the media realm – and were militia friendly. If there was one thing the freedom movement needed, it was a press capable of reaching people with the message. Rampaging Elephants was also a big supporter of the Texas independence movement. There should be some useful contacts to come from that event even if nothing else happened.

The meeting drew in a good sample of the militia units across the state. Many of the pure survivalists or resistor types of what Roberts referred to as the guerrilla groups did not show. He was impressed with the morning host from Rampaging Elephants and the retired general the host had invited. The general emphasized the importance of paying attention to the tasks that did not involve shooting. In Roberts view, anybody who didn't get on board with what the general had to say was an idiot. Unfortunately, that seemed to account for 80% of the attendees who were group leaders.

At least Roberts was now connected to Rampaging Elephants and the general, which would do for a start. If any of the militias ever decided to focus on anything other than trying to subsume every other militia in the state into their command structure, and everybody in the unit jumping up and out from cover, running toward targets while shooting, we might get somewhere. Until, then, Roberts would work with what was there. Most importantly was to work within the framework the general and Rampaging

Elephants host had in mind. He had found some smart people with the rudiments of a plan.

The meeting went about as Roberts had expected. Pledges to cooperate without any foundation for cross communication or plan to create communications capability. Some schoolyard puffery and bloviating as to which groups don't like each other, combined with exaggerated claims about unit strength and abilities. It was fairly typical of the freedom movement – a number of strong personalities unable to cooperate with each other.

The general had spoken about the ability to shape events and identify points at which pressure to influence political opinion could be applied, thus allowing in many cases for substituting the application of force. Roberts was happy to hear that because he knew he could trust the general in this environment. There was an understanding of how this had to work, the military having been exposed to the Iraq and Afghanistan conflicts had learned that pure military force application has limitations when trying to achieve political ends.

Roberts and the general spoke briefly after the meeting. "I'm happy to see you in this sir. The only chance there is of getting some cooperation between groups is an outside leader. Those that won't follow your advice will probably be too stupid to be useful."

"What have we really got in terms of capability?"

"Field strength is maybe a battalion, if you took all of the groups and consolidated them to get real units. Big problem is no logistics and no communications capability. Combat support non existent, due to lack of awareness and no way to get real equipment. Most units would be done in 24 hours one way or the other. No concept of information operations. As for leadership, you saw it in action today."

"Looked like dealing with World War II re-enactors."

"Had not thought of it that way, sir. But that probably is a good parallel. Of course, we don't operate that way. We actually have a training plan and a METL. We still suck, just not as much as the others. We have some communications gear and field ranges for preparing meals. We could last a week if nothing happens."

The general grinned. "Captain, you have just been assigned the additional duty of being the entire staff, in addition to your command. You OK with that?"

"Yes sir, but if the others find out that I'm the guy writing all of this stuff, that will come back on you."

"I know."

Roberts also found the Rampaging Elephants morning host very personable, smart, and able to check his ego at the door to enable getting something done. Qualities that were all in short supply in the freedom movement and a bonus to find them in one man. Roberts decided he needed to pay more attention to the host, and listen in to Rampaging Elephants whenever possible.

The meeting went into the plus column as far as Roberts was concerned. He had made two good contacts, another couple of maybes, and a couple of militia units that had not talked to other units showed up. Having some friends to help out certainly beats trying to do things alone.

Not long after the meeting, the Rampaging Elephants morning host had a guest on his program from the Free Texas organization. There were a number of Texas independence organizations, and it seemed that most of the leadership of Free Texas had split from the Native Texan Movement. The Free Texas representative was interesting, as he was articulate and was laying out the plan Free Texas was authoring in order to transition Texas from a state to a republic. Unlike with most of these groups, Free Texas was presenting a serious transition plan that showed some people with some intellect had worked this out. Roberts decided that Free Texas merited more of his attention to see what was going on there. These people were serious about working out how to do it.

This had the potential to align nicely with a concept that Roberts had been working on for a while. Libertarians had been preaching for years on something they called the Free State Project. The idea being that all libertarians move to a state and start voting for less government and more freedom. The idea was sound, but as with most schemes like this, the execution of the plan was lacking. The problem essentially was, OK I move there and then what? People need housing, jobs, and a decent economy already in place or reasonably certain in order to take the degree of risk involved in a move.

Roberts thought the better prospect for success would be to start small and work up. Let the additional people and politics become the follow on effects from existing success. The power of a positive example is more inspiring, and more likely to motivate people to act, than a great sounding idea. The idea was right, but the scale was too large. It could be done at the county level, and Texas was a just about perfect venue for the plan. In previous times, a dissatisfied population would leave for the frontier and create their own settlements. That was not possible in the 21st

Century, but something similar was possible in a county with a small population.

Essentially, the federal government is the same across the country. Everyone is subject to those officials enforcing their edicts, so in which state one resides is immaterial relative to interaction with the federal government. States have a wide degree of latitude in laws and regulations. Some states are far more restrictive than others. Some states have by law or tradition, a very high degree of home rule – meaning the state does little beyond defining crimes and most government activity happens at the county or town level. Roberts thought Texas was pretty good on his scale of power toward the local rather than state level.

At the state level the only things every Texan had to deal with was your car – license, inspection and state required insurance. A land owner could have state level interaction for well drilling. A problem in Texas was special purpose districts such as water conservation, improvement, and other sweetheart deals, but there were counties without such things. One might be in a licensed occupation, and that would be another state interaction. There was a state mandated minimum property tax level for schools, but that was about it. Individuals did not spend much time dealing with the State of Texas under normal circumstances.

In reality, most interaction was at the county or town level. Property taxes were collected by the county. A couple of percent of the sales tax went to the town. Things like building codes, food prep, traffic, and so on were primarily town matters. Many of the urban counties had the county see revenue opportunities existing by doing some of these things at the county level, but that was not the case in rural Texas. By carefully choosing the county in which one lived, many minor irritants in life could be eliminated. The tradeoff was that you were living alone in the middle of nowhere.

Extending the thought to its logical conclusion, a small number of people who formed a substantial percentage of the population of a county would determine who filled the following offices; sheriff, county attorney, county commissioners, school board, county tax collector, constable, and so on. If you controlled those offices, you controlled to some degree the tax rate on property, school instruction, how much police you wanted, and what crimes you wanted prosecuted or not. District Court judges in Texas are elected, thus you could also get rid of a judge who did not get it right. A Texas county controlled by a number of freedom minded individuals seemed like an exciting prospect for someone determined to lead a life of liberty.

The question is what incentive is needed to get some freedom minded individuals to make the move. Roberts decided the reason why the free state project was not working was because the people follow the jobs. The plan needed to be sold not to freedom loving individuals, but to people who could start or move existing businesses and employ people. If low taxes are good for individuals, they do no harm to a business either. Roberts needed to find people who would move or start small businesses in a low regulation environment, at least relatively speaking. The hope would be that freedom oriented small business owners would employ a like minded work force. This would skew the vote even more toward more freedom.

One of the issues created by a service based economy, rather than a manufacturing economy, is that some businesses need an existing population base in order to be viable. That would initially limit the business base upon which the concept could be built. But once under way, it would feed on itself. The key was to make a start and get something going. Roberts expected that this would eventually become one or more communities, and then the concept would expand to other counties.

And there was one more wrinkle to the plan that Roberts was keeping to himself. Part of identifying the people needed for the plan was the need to defend the community that would be built. As the community grew, there would be two issues that would have to be managed. Eventually, a town would be created, and the temptation to impose controls on people and levy taxes would have to be fought. The town would have to live on sales tax revenue while growing.

There was one aspect even more important – flying low under the radar of not being in an urban environment, meant that there were good odds that obnoxious federal regulations could probably be ignored with success. This could not go on forever, and at some future time, a federal agency would come to visit and seek to impose its will.

This would create conflict that would be the defining moment in which liberty would continue to be restored or crushed. Roberts expected the people of this community to be part of the local militia, and when this conflict occurred, it would be the duty of the militia to defend the community from the invasion. In a sense, this would be a pre planned Bundy Ranch scenario. The goal would be to force the federal government to back down from imposing an edict on the community that the community refused to obey.

That community would defy anyone to take our liberty, and this would forever change ourselves, Texas, the United States, and possibly the world.

To do this required a special breed of people, and Texas was the place to find them. It seemed that they tended to gather in Free Texas, and that would be the place to pitch the plan.

Chapter 5

Meetings

As a rule, Roberts hated meetings, but this one would be different and not just because he was the one putting it together. This meeting could be the opportunity that would really get the ball rolling in making a real and lasting change in their lives, the lives of millions of Texans, and possibly the United States as well. If he would be able to persuade some people to make real changes in their lives, and put up the capital to do it, nothing would be the same going forward. The library's meeting room wasn't quite filled when the 11 participants were all present, but bigger movements had started with less.

Roberts opened the meeting "First, I thank all of you for attending and your willingness to listen to this plan. What I have is a general outline, and subject to modification as each of you has experience to contribute, and our success will depend on how many people are willing to risk change. Never easy, but the potential rewards are great.

All great ideas are simple at their core, and this one is no different. Many of us are tired of the current political and economic landscape. We don't need the details as you already know them. As individuals, there is next to nothing we can do to effect meaningful change. We have voted as hard as we can, but our voice is lost in the din. There is a way to change that. Our ancestors had vast unsettled territories to flee to and set up those systems of government they thought would suit their needs. That option is closed to us. Or is it?"

At that point he got a bit more attention.

Roberts continued "Texas has several counties that have lost population over the past decades. We can move people to a low population county, where our numbers will favorably impact the way in which we live. If done properly we will make friends with those already there, who for the most part, will see things as we do. Once they are convinced that we are there to lead lives of freedom and prosperity, our additional numbers will grow the local economy and I think they will be true allies in what we are about.

We can elect a sheriff who will follow the Constitution, a District Attorney who will stay within the bounds of his office, keep taxes low by electing the county officials, and certainly not least, a school board that will trash the new curriculum and bring back education that will teach our children to really be able to read, to learn to think, develop an appreciation of freedom, and be productive citizens. We all remember the places in which we grew up as children, and we can recover that life once again.

What it takes is for us to agree on which county in which we wish to settle, and then move our lives there. As we experience success, more of those who think like we do will be willing to move there and then the idea will spread to other counties. It is a chance to make the political system work for us instead of being overwhelmed by it in the urban environment."

That started the dialog.

Ted Greenlow was the first to ask "Where are you thinking about? All of those counties are in the middle of nowhere. Nobody wants to move there." Greenlow was linked to a more urban setting as he was in sales and it would be difficult to build a new customer base somewhere else. It would be difficult on him to move.

Roberts replied "I'm proposing Borden County. The current population is 641. Two counties, or over an hour's drive away is Lubbock. Everybody that lives in the Houston or Dallas / Ft. Worth areas already can have almost as much drive time to get to somewhere anyway. So, a good size town is not too far away, but far enough away that we can avoid over crowding. The county seat is Gail, population 231, and that has the school district for the county. There are some empty stores and a few homes in the area that can do for a start. The school district has just over one teacher per grade with an enrollment of 239.

There is a city water system, or go independent via a well. There are several electric companies and co-ops. Land tends to run less than $2000 per acre. And it is not like there are city building codes or anything like that.

It isn't as if there wouldn't be any business opportunities there, especially if we make our own. One opportunity would be to develop a couple of hundred acres into a housing development, use the profit from selling lots to put in roads and water lines by selling quarter acre lots for what you paid for an acre. It may start off looking like a Gypsy camp, but as the area develops, housing will improve."

Ed McMasters was the next questioner "What else do you think could make it out there?" McMasters make a decent income from rental real estate, so the development had his interest.

Roberts replied "As for me personally, I've wanted to start an ammunition plant. Not just reloading on steroids, but real deal military spec manufacturing. The guys who re-engineered the Lake City Army Ammunition Plant do consulting, and they make production machines. Not the sort of thing I could locate in the middle of a town, and I figure there will be a constant market for ammunition as things continue to go bad, and the occasional panic buying along the way. Problem is that it puts the ATF in my life at some time in the future, but as it won't be some huge operation, I might not be that high on their radar.

Another play is technology. Because schools are wired in, there will be some net connectivity that could allow for either remote workers to move in, or some business to base there – it would have a synergistic effect if we can get some of the Texas independence organizations to start operating from the Territory of Free Texas, which is not a bad name for the project.

But there has to be somebody here smarter than I am who could operate a business there. And this brings up another key point. Once we start creating jobs, we heed to hire people that we already know that are liberty minded. First, this will help make and keep the local government under a proper constitutional foundation. More importantly, we need to keep our community helpful of each other like good neighbors. Because the people we hire will be our neighbors, and character matters.

Look at what happens to a community of any size. It gets a convenience store, then cafes, leading to a general store, grocery store. The prosperity feeds on itself. In an area where property is not that easy to buy, those who get to move in become those that the people in the already existing community welcome."

"What are the politics like?" one of the other attendees asked Roberts.

"Last election, 439 voters, 260 voted in the last election and it voted 90% Republican. It is a matter of seeing how many of those Republicans are really willing to stand up for liberty. In the worst case, we will outnumber them in the Republican Primary in short order. It may take a surprise contested primary to do it, but not hard for a motivated small group to do." Roberts responded.

"Have you checked the price of land?" inquired someone else.

"About $2000 an acre, it obviously costs more in town." answered Roberts.

"We could get to a situation where those already there start to feel displaced, and that might be a bit tough." Ted Greenlow was at least thinking it over.

Roberts commented "That is an important point. We should be sending the message that we are moving there not to really change the place, but to build decent lives for ourselves. That stress will probably occur once we get about 100 people in. That means an impact on schools, and the existing infrastructure. If we make a point of paying our own way in infrastructure improvements that should generate some goodwill. A few more kids in the schools will mean more state money, and that should be seen by the current residents as a plus.

The tipping point will be if we need to replace elected officials that will not be supportive of what we are doing. That activity needs to be carefully targeted. These places have large land owning families, and they will be concerned that this will cost them money or control. Some like being county officials to control things, other officials are there just because nobody else is there to do the job. We will have to be very careful and deliberate as to which positions we target and people we replace."

"Any other ideas?" Ed McMasters asked.

"Remote technology related things could work. Wiring schools to the internet means that there should be some high bandwidth network in the county seat that could be connected to in order to leverage off of that. People with experience in different areas may have even better ideas." suggested Roberts.

"What do we do to get this moving?" Ed was interested in the plan.

"Buy some land out there and then we should get together and see what might be the priority of work." Roberts said.

"How many people do you think it will take to make this work?" McMasters continued to think out loud.

"We will probably need at least 5 buying in with land purchases. That is the first part requiring some capital, or at least financing for the parcel that does not get subdivided for housing. Assuming some workforce, or people with some disposable income to buy a lot, we are looking anywhere from some 50 to 100, and by the time you add family members, we are going to have a community of 200 plus that should grow from there. That growth will feed on itself with a general store, café, and we will probably incorporate a town." Roberts stated.

"A town?" Ed had not thought that would be part of the plan.

Roberts reasoned "Mainly as a pre-emptive strike so as not to get annexed at some time in the future, plus that will probably facilitate a water system. And there may be some other benefits by being a government entity. That can be decided when we get there. As much as I hate to say it, it is a financing system for infrastructure via a sales tax. I'm libertarian, but using a government mechanism to do economy of scale activities makes some sense. We just don't make it mandatory for the citizenry to pay for services not used."

"Doesn't that put the state in our business?" Ed asked.

Roberts had done some research. "Same idea as with the pre-emptive city thinking. Any water system with 24 or more connections is supposed to be inspected by the state. As long as that is not a problem which would cause us to do something that we would not do otherwise, we may play within the rules when it is to our advantage, then it may not be so obvious when we break the rules."

Chapter 6

Insurgents

The directors of Free Texas were making changes to the board. One of the board members resigned and the number of directors was being expanded to five. The result was that there were now two open positions awaiting appointment. Roberts had been attending meetings for a few months and had met two of the board members. He had also written a couple of editorials designed to benefit the organization.

Es McMasters, one of the board members called Roberts, "Are you free for dinner tomorrow?"

"Sure, where do you want to meet?" Roberts agreed

Ed was happy with the response. "I can come toward you." They agreed on location and time.

Roberts figured that he had been selected for some project on behalf of Free Texas. Roberts liked the organization and the board members he had met. These guys had come to the conclusion that the US was heading for collapse or break up, and while the whole country could not be saved, at least Texas could be saved. They had been working on a transition plan, and it was for real, not the incoherent ramblings of dreamers.

Traffic was bad and Roberts was ten minutes late. "Sorry about being late, that is something that really annoys me."

"No problem. Have you guessed why I asked you to meet?" Ed asked.

"I assume there is something you think that I can do for Free Texas, in addition to being a member." replied Roberts

Ed brought up the issue. "There is. As you probably know, we had a board member resign due to health reasons, and we need a replacement. We think that you are the right one for the job of replacing him."

"As you may already know, I'm the leader of a militia, some organizations in the political realm consider that a major liability." Roberts wasn't going to take a chance or the organization having a surprise because of his other activities.

"We have no problem with that at all. We support the militia movement." Ed told Roberts.

"In that case, I am flattered and accept the offer. I have a couple of current things I'll need to unwind to really get going, but I believe in what Free Texas is doing and look forward to trying to help out some more." Roberts now had one more volunteer job.

"That is what I was hoping you would say. One of the great things about Free Texas is there very little ego involved on the part of the leaders and also at the county level. What we are doing is too important for that." Ed continued.

"I've noticed, and that is another thing I like about Free Texas. Practically everybody is focused on the task." Roberts noted.

Dinner is much more pleasant when it is good news all the way around thought Roberts. The challenge would be to make Free Texas into a movement that would influence events in the state of Texas. That was just the sort of thing he would find interesting and exciting.

Roberts was thinking in terms of the insurgency part of Irregular Warfare, defined thus by Army FM 3-05.130 (2008) "In contrast, IW focuses on the control or influence of populations, not on the control of an adversary's forces or territory. Ultimately, IW is a political struggle with violent and nonviolent components. The struggle is for control or influence over and the support of a relevant population. The foundation for IW is the centrality of the relevant populations to the nature of the conflict. The parties to an IW conflict, whether states or armed groups, seek to undermine their adversaries' legitimacy and credibility. They seek to physically and psychologically isolate their adversaries from the relevant populations and their external supporters. At the same time, they also seek to bolster their own legitimacy and credibility to exercise authority over that same population."

Roberts had the good fortune that in this case, it seemed every level of government in the United States was working diligently to undermine its own legitimacy with the majority of Americans. That makes the job the insurgents so much easier. That is what makes an insurgency campaign possible. After all, Roberts and his associates were part of that population with which those governments were losing legitimacy by violating the supreme law of the land, and not operating within its limitations. Of the seven phases of an Irregular Warfare campaign, Roberts considered that he was already at Phase IV, and had yet to get seriously started.

The insurgency is organized into three components according to Army Unconventional Warfare doctrine:

"(1) Guerrillas represent the most commonly recognized portion of the insurgency. They are a group of irregular, predominantly indigenous personnel organized along military lines to conduct paramilitary operations in enemy-held, hostile, or denied territory. Guerrillas carry out most of the armed conflict that openly challenges the regional authority." Being able to form a militia meant that Roberts had already begun the transition from irregulars to conventional force, which happens as the insurgents are successful in winning.

(2) "The auxiliary is the primary support element of the irregular organization whose organization and operations are clandestine in nature and whose members do not openly indicate their sympathy or involvement with the irregular movement. This support enables the guerrilla force—and often the underground—to survive and function. This support can take the form of logistics, labor, or intelligence.

Although many functions of the auxiliary and underground overlap, auxiliaries are more likely in rural environments where the relative distance and dispersion of adversary forces permit operations by guerrilla or other armed irregular forces. Members of the auxiliary are sometimes characterized as "part-time members" of the irregular organization, continuing to participate in the life of their community—to all appearances concerned only with their normal occupations—and at the same time engaging in irregular operations to varying degrees. Local cell or element leaders organize and coordinate all efforts, which the area or sector command directs. These various elements may serve as support cells within compartmentalized support networks." Free Texas was perfectly positioned to do this.

(3) "The underground is a cellular organization within the irregular movement that is responsible for subversion, sabotage, intelligence collection, and other compartmentalized activities. Most underground operations are required to take place in and around population centers. As such, the underground must have the ability to conduct operations in areas that are usually inaccessible to the guerrillas, such as areas under government military control. Underground members often fill leadership positions, overseeing specific functions that auxiliary workers carry out. The underground and auxiliary—although technically separate units— are, in reality, loosely connected elements that provide coordinated capabilities for the irregular movement. The key distinction between them is that the underground is the element of the irregular organization that operates in areas denied to the guerrilla force."

At its core elements, the plan was simple. Roberts would use US Special Forces Unconventional Warfare doctrine to restore liberty to Texas, if not the United States. Insurgencies shared certain characteristics. The government forces generally had control of urban areas, and the insurgents were forced out into the countryside. The insurgents tried to establish rural bases and gain the confidence and support of the rural population. While there was a political struggle for legitimacy in the eyes of the population, government entities would conduct operations to attempt to find and eliminate the insurgents.

The immediate goal of the insurgents was to gain control over rural areas, turning them into "no go" zones for hostile government entities. A successful insurgency over time, expands its zone of control until reaching urban areas. As urban areas are dependent on transportation of food, energy, and goods from those rural areas, the insurgents then work to cut these vital supplies to urban areas. Being able to do this successfully, further serves to make the existing government seem ineffective, and lose more legitimacy in the eyes of the urban population by failing to meet their needs. Thus, the urban population is prepared to support an alternative to the existing government.

There were a couple of unique aspects to the situation that fell outside of Army doctrine. Most insurgencies have support from an external source. This activity was self directed. The other big difference was that there was no intention to overthrow the existing governmental institutions. Roberts figured that the ever increasing number of socialists and their policies would take care of the loss of government legitimacy and failure to meet the needs of a substantial percentage of the population for him. It was helpful to have an opponent who had no idea that he was in the middle of an insurgency. All he had to do was position himself for taking advantage of an opportunity when it was presented.

Now it was time to get to work and set the plan in motion.

Ed McMasters made a fair amount of money as a landlord and from real estate deals. He took a look at buying a tract of land for the purpose of subdivision into lots for sale to individuals for housing. He also had contacts with builders and construction workers. Many of the militia members in Roberts militia also had building and construction experience. The goal was to be close to the county seat of Gail which initially would allow for both settlements to use the same retail and food service, while maintaining enough distance to be separate communities. The other goal was a tract size of over 100 acres, but less than 200 acres, which would be subdivided into quarter acre lots, and leave some room for the water system, and limited retail or business use.

Next, consideration was given to incorporating as a Type C general law city. That type of city would require a mayor and two council members, have elections and observe the required bidding process for contracts. The advantage would be the ability to prevent annexation by any other entity, and the residents could set their own price for utilities. The city would be limited to the ability to tax property up to 25 cents per $100 value per year. As there was no intention to have a property tax anyway, the lower the legal limit the better. It made sense to go ahead with the city incorporation, on the theory that nobody would really care much about what happened in some small town in the middle of nowhere. The risk to be managed was a council that might want to use government code authority to start acting like a larger city.

The understanding with McMasters was to use $1000 from each lot sale to fund the town. This would provide for a water system, and buy two one acre plots – one for the town center and water tower, and the other for water treatment. The town center plot was retained and only the fenced water tower and park area was donated, and the rest of the acre would be more valuable as commercial area. That led to the logical layout of the streets, which would be around the town square and run past each of the quarter acre lots. Freedonia, Texas was now in business as soon as the county approved the incorporation.

Roberts thought Texas needed an ammunition plant. Not massive reloading type production, but to military specifications. He had found the company that did the retooling of the Lake City Army Ammunition Plant, and decided that replicating that process was what he wanted to do. With one production line, an eight hour shift could turn out about 25,000 rounds of 5.56mm M193 or M855 ball, or the same machines could turn out 7.62mm M80 ball. The same machines could also be used for M856 or M62 tracer if needed. Just the assembly to add the sealant at the primer base and case neck required two specialized machines.

The next priority for production would be the machines needed to make brass cases, as these cases were expensive to buy new, and production with a unique headstamp on the case would be a good way to brand the product. The next biggest cost item to internalize would be to make projectiles. After that, would be primer production. They were cheap as a cost component of the round, but far worse would be not to be able to get any during the periodic ammunition buying panics. The toughest item to manufacture would be powder. It was a cheap component and needed complex infrastructure to produce, being the result of a chemical manufacturing process. Well, the journey of a thousand miles starts with a singe step. No matter how far down the production chain the plant went, there would always be the need for a reliable supply of raw materials in some form.

While organizing this, there was time to wait on the ATF to approve his license to manufacture ammunition. Or, if they didn't, the project would drive on anyway, and possibly even engage one of the Second Amendment friendly lawyers around the gun rights movement for some fun. Just exactly how large of an operation Roberts had in mind was left unclear. Also not mentioned were some "black" projects that were in the mind of Roberts for which the ammunition plant would serve as a cover. If for some reason he got real ambitious, he could try for an Army additional source contract. With Lake City being the only plant in the country to make ammunition for the military, they would occasionally contract with other suppliers to maintain the industrial base. As

Freedonia, was much closer to the western Army ammunition depot in Utah, than was the Lake City plant being in Missouri, he would have an advantage in cost of shipping.

All of this would serve as a base for moving the militia to Borden County. Members that needed jobs, would work at the plant, or on the construction of the homes and buildings that would become Freedonia, and its surroundings. Other jobs would be offered to members of Free Texas, with the understanding that part of the job was membership in the Borden County Militia.

Other small business owners were encouraged to consider moving operations to the Freedonia area or elsewhere in the county. The scheme also worked for those tied to larger cities because of the nature of their employment. They could buy a lot in Freedonia, and then build a residence as money was available, many working on weekends. More importantly, Freedonia was now the legal residence for them and their families. Soon, Freedonia had over 200 registered voters, a school bus load of kids, and at over 25% population growth in one year, was located in the fastest growing county in Texas.

Roberts, McMasters, Greenlow, and the other business owners made a point of being seen around Gail at the school board meetings, and the county commissioners meetings. It was important that the existing residents get to know the key players in Freedonia so as to ensure relations in the county were friendly with everyone there. Of course, the residents of Freedonia were taking the measure of the ground and evaluating the personalities comprising the government of the county, the sheriff and the county attorney. They needed to assess who would be friendly to what they had in mind, who would be neutral, and who would be hostile.

Chapter 7

The Bank that Wasn't

A vibrant community ends up with some type of financial services institution. One that safely stores money, makes loans, and facilitates transactions. Roberts decided that the time had come to start such an institution in Freedonia, but governments and existing financial institutions were keen on preventing just anyone from buying and installing a safe, booting up a computer, and opening a retail location and calling that entity a bank. There were rules about that sort of thing. Even a State Bank chartered by the State of Texas required $5 million in capital, 11 stockholders, and an application stating the proposed location, community to be served, and other information that the authorities may or may not find acceptable. A Community Thrift could be done in theory with just $1 million in capital, but many of the same regulations would apply. Roberts had neither the money, nor the inclination to fool with all of that. In any case, being a "legitimate" financial services business was not part of the bigger plan.

What was needed to start the operation was a safe. The valuables have to be kept somewhere. And a computer was needed to keep the list of account holders and balances. Then, the Freedonia Transaction Company needed a place to do business. As the community was growing, the last of the three was proving to be the most difficult. Roberts debated even about sending in the $300 to the Texas Secretary of State to register the corporation, but decided the advantages out weighed the disadvantages. Ultimately, a plot of land in what was the community of Freedonia, which elsewhere might be referred to as a city block, became the commercial center, with storefronts along two streets. One of these storefronts became the Freedonia Transaction Company. The bylaws sent in with the registration to the Secretary of State was an exercise in taking up pages of paper to obfuscate what the company was really going to do. In reality, for the most part the State of Texas really didn't care why you wanted to start a business, so the registration was completed in a few days.

This operation was going to be critical, and the right person for the job was an imperative. Roberts knew exactly who he needed for this task. Beth Dunwoody was somewhat known in the patriot community. She first gained notoriety by posting a Youtube video of herself reading some of the more offensive parts of the Koran, using strips of bacon to bookmark the extremely offensive passages she quoted in the video. Beth had owned a business related to financial services, but shut down the business while warning her clients of impending financial collapse, advising them to get all financial assets out of exposure to stock and commodities market risk now.

On top of that, the IRS considered her a tax resistor for her refusing to finance the engine of evil and oppression. The IRS swooped in and took her home and anything else it could confiscate. Beth did not cave in under pressure, and Roberts considered it likely that before this was over, the Freedonia Transaction Company would come to the attention of certain authorities and the person running the show on location would have an unpleasant encounter with people wearing badges and carrying firearms.

The challenge Roberts faced here would be to convince Beth that he was serious about her running this operation. Her internet persona indicated that she did not have a generally high opinion of most people in the freedom movement. Roberts could sympathize with that. Most people are not willing to take risks, even moderate risk, as long as they are reasonably comfortable. Jefferson put it best "accordingly all experience hath shewn, that mankind are more disposed to suffer, while evils are sufferable, than to right themselves by abolishing the forms to which they are accustomed." However, people also respond to effective leadership. It was the job of Roberts, McMasters, Greenlow, and the rest of the Free Texas directors to provide that leadership.

The first issue would be to get Dunwoody to respond to his email, as she probably would not take the offer seriously. He knew she wouldn't be interested in running a conventional financial services organization. He would have to appeal to the uniqueness of the concept behind the Freedonia Transaction Company. It would essentially be a precious metals US coinage bank treating US paper currency issued by the Federal Reserve as a foreign currency. This would position the bank to be able to transition to Texas independence and the notional Texas dollar (TXD) by observing the principles of a sound money regime.

If a way could be found to get into the international SWIFT payment system, and one or more of the credit card networks, that would be a bonus. That would also allow for an interface between the sound currency to be used by the Freedonia Transaction Company with the current US currency and financial systems. This would make it easier for customers to be paid in sound money and conduct any necessary transactions outside of the sound money financial system in which the Freedonia Transaction Company would play a key part. Thus, the US government paper dollar would be treated just as if it was any other foreign currency.

Roberts thought this would appeal to Dunwoody if he could just get through to her and have a serious conversation. People with her courage and conviction were rare and are hard to find. She was perfect for this operation. Roberts sent the email outlining the plan and asked if she would be willing to be part of the operation. Then he waited to receive a response. If that failed, he would have to find someone else with a financial industry background for the task. As most of the people with those qualifications were afraid of the IRS and what the IRS could do to their ability to operate in the industry, it would be a real tough nut to crack if Dunwoody had no interest in the offer.

Fortunately a reply came and it was positive. Dunwoody was interested in the happenings in Freedonia and Borden County. However, her interest pointed out one problem in the plan. There was no temporary housing anywhere in the county. That was by design as visitors were generally discouraged, but that would be more and more of an issue as the community grew and people needed some time to settle in. Maybe the time had come for a small group of studio apartments. Yet another investment opportunity had been found.

With someone now on the way to run the operation, the plan could proceed. The bank would be run from a series of Excel spreadsheets kept on a USB drive, and backed up to another USB drive. With both USB drives encrypted, just who had what on deposit or on loan from the bank would not easily find its way to China, or Washington, DC for that matter. The Freedonia

Transaction Company would be an exercise in bank secrecy. It would be bank procedure to keep the USB in the safe, and then open the safe to conduct a major transaction using the USB in a laptop, and then lock the USB again in the safe. At the end of the month, statements could be printed out for all of the account holders. The other bank secret would be the ability of the manager to send a distress call to Roberts and the Borden County Militia in case uninvited guests with guns arrived.

Roberts thought that such a visit well could be in the future of the FTC. A great deal of cash would go through it as a conduit of money in and out of Freedonia. Most everyday transactions were cash, only the land deals were still using the US financial system, and that meant that without entry into the ABA clearinghouse system, there would be a number of cash transactions that would come to the attention of other banks, and thus to the IRS. One of the challenges Dunwoody would face was to try to find an outside of the US bank that would front for the Freedonia Transaction Company.

As long as financing remained local, all would be well, but until that could happen, the residents of Freedonia were linked to the national financial system, and that meant risk associated with financial collapse or government action. Neither was pleasant to contemplate. Freedonia needed independence from the US financial system, and that was the main task of the Freedonia Transaction Company. Like any other bank, a strong Fredonia Transaction Company could lend the capital needed for the development of the town. Success would then feed on itself and expand the community.

Chapter 8

To Coin Money and Regulate the Value Thereof

Part of the ability to control a country or its people is the control of the money that the population uses to conduct business. It was something the financial services industry knew all too well. With the creation of the Federal Reserve System, the banking industry of the United States had hit the mother lode. Especially so as later in the 20th Century, US power became world wide in influence and reach. The Federal Reserve created money from nothing, loaned it at a favorable rate of interest to commercial banks, who then made loans to consumers, business or as became fashionable post 2008, took money at almost zero interest to buy Treasury bonds, speculate in the markets themselves, or any other number of "funny money" schemes. Post 2008, such was the case with 85% of the money banks borrowed from the Fed. Only 15% went into the economy as financing to other businesses and individuals. None of these things benefited the economy (except for commercial bank profitability), and created a house of cards that would wipe out most of the individual wealth of the working people of the country when it happened. Roberts had been to MBA School and knew how the game was played.

The key to preserving individual wealth and the ability to increase the same, depended on not being tied to that ship when it went down. The way that disaster is avoided is with sound money, meaning money based on silver and gold coins. If anything else is used as money, whoever issues that money will at some point give in to the temptation to cheat on the metal content of the coinage. That is one of the lessons of history. Silver and gold coins work as a store of value. In 1964, two silver dimes could buy a gallon of gas. Those two 1964 silver dimes still could buy a gallon of gas 50 years later. An economy based on silver coinage could insulate the community from financial collapse to some degree. Or, any other chicanery that anyone in the financial system had in mind. The goal was to stop using money that had no value other than the notional value that the US Government said it did. The full faith and credit of the United States meant nothing to those who had no faith in the government's credit.

Various schemes had been tried before based on precious metals, and the IRS had shut them all down. The answer to that problem was to use US coinage, as there could be no doubt that the money to be used was minted by the US government. The idea is that it would be hard for the US government to deny that coins that it had produced were a legal currency. Particularly hard to deny that they are currency when those coins were defined as legal tender by the Coinage Act of 1965. Minting non coins, or tokens from silver was where the others had gone off track in Roberts view. As long as a silver dollar produced by the US government was a dollar, the plan would work.

58

US Courts had found gold contracts legal in the early 2000s, and that was the key. All transactions and contracts would specify payment in silver in those dealings with which Roberts exercised control. Other members of the Freedonia community had stores of precious metals, mostly silver US coins known as junk silver, other coins, and silver minted pieces from various sources. Roberts asked around as to why wait for the collapse to switch to a silver based system when we could do that now.

Roberts was already doing so with the people who worked in his businesses. He structured jobs so that the people could be employed as contractors, including himself. The people had an option – work for Federal Reserve Notes, the standard US currency, or have a contract specifying payment in silver. Roberts did the same with every transaction he could. As he explained the concept:

"If I asked you to work for me all day for a piece of paper with Alexander Hamilton's picture on it that said ten dollars, would you do it? Probably not. If I asked you to work all day for me for ten silver coins minted by the US Government, each claiming the value of one dollar, would you do it? Either way, I am going to give you an IRS Form 1099 at the end of the year that says you got ten dollars in income from me."

"But Roberts, you are taking an accounting loss by paying in silver." Ed McMasters was intrigued how Roberts intended for the plan to work.

"Short term I am, but it reduces taxable profit, and the more people I can get to buy in to the plan, my income and expenses reduce as well. The goal is to get income below the level that requires the payment of tax." Roberts explained.

"Why hasn't this been tried before?" Ed asked.

"Variations of it have, but those attempts were managed badly. You can't have it both ways. You can't tell the IRS you have an income of $5000 per year, and then go apply for a credit card claiming an income of $75,000 per year based on the value of the silver. That is the problem having our own financial institution solves. People can get credit in silver, based on silver contract income. The Transaction Company can extent to you $1000 TXD in silver dollars as a loan, which you can convert to Federal Reserve Notes like any other foreign currency, and then buy a car.

The other thing that trapped previous operators, was minting their own silver one ounce or part of an ounce coins and claiming they were bartering or using currency terms like dollar. This plan only uses US Government minted coins. This will put the government in the position of either being unable to stop it, or having to claim a one dollar coin minted by the US Government is not a dollar, but something else. Hard to do when you go to a bank with a roll of $10 in silver quarters and walk away with a piece of paper with Alexander Hamilton's picture on it." Roberts further explained the concept.

"How do you work it in practice?" continued McMasters.

"Everything I do has two prices. The constant silver price that never varies, and the spot price in US Dollars (USD) based on the price of silver. You will always get a better deal from me paying in silver. Notionally, I call the silver price the Texas Dollar (TXD). When people ask me about the lower price and how to get it, I have the opportunity to explain how the government has cheated them out of their money by inflating the currency. My prices are the same as they were in 1950." answered Roberts.

"If this really takes off can we get enough silver coins to use everywhere? Won't we run out of sources for US coins?" Ed was now more curious.

"Potentially, the supply of US minted coinage might get tight, but that is one of the tasks of the Transaction Company, to balance the need in the community for silver and Federal Reserve Notes. Using the Federal Notes to obtain silver coinage at favorable exchange rates, just like any international bank does. It can also do one other useful thing. Just like banks did before the Federal Reserve, the Transaction Company can issue Promissory Notes redeemable in silver coinage. The note will contain the wording 'The Freedonia Transaction Company promises to pay the bearer on demand, One Dollar in silver' which you can at any time redeem for a silver dollar at the Transaction Company. This saves you the trouble of having to carry around ten pounds of coins, and reduces wear on the old coins we have which can be kept in the safe as the currency reserve." Roberts further elaborated.

"This has got to annoy the IRS and they will do something about it." Ed concluded.

Roberts was prepared with the answer. "Eventually, I expect that it will. You asked me about what all of this stuff we are doing had with achieving Texas independence. While it will be great that we are freer than before, Texas independence may be the main goal. Here is the link. We keep pushing the envelope of freedom. If the feds do nothing, we become more free. If we provoke a reaction, we create a conflict in which the people of Texas have to choose sides. Choosing our side will result in either an independent Texas, or a return to a federal system of government as set up by our founders.

If they have to react to actions we take, we have the advantage. I am of the opinion that if we create actual liberty on the ground, the politics will follow. I am aware that the other groups want to work the politics first, and then put the economic mechanisms in place. The fact that they have made little progress in ten to twenty years of effort has caused me to think of another approach as being more likely to obtain a favorable result."

"Brilliant. You seem to have the answer for everything." Ed remarked.

"I don't, but the careful study of history provides evidence for what works and does not work under similar circumstances. That makes a good point from which to start and then learn from actual experience." summarized Roberts.

"So you are saying that in a real sense the 1776 Declaration of Independence was the end result of having already become independent, not a statement of intending to do so?" Ed got the historical point.

"Exactly, and having control over your own money is an imperative for independence as an individual or as a nation." Roberts agreed.

Soon thereafter, currency printed by the US Federal Reserve banks was a rare sight in Freedonia. If the Freedonia Transaction Company could not obtain an ABA routing number because it had no bank charter, other non US banks were not so hesitant to do business with the Freedonia Transaction Company. The Freedonia Transaction Company opened a corporate account with a US branch of a foreign bank that did not do consumer business in the US. Customers of the Freedonia Transaction Company had the opportunity to have a Visa card for TXD with the logo of the Freedonia Transaction Company. Behind the scenes, the transactions were actually processed by a bank in Lithuania, the bill paid to the Freedonia Transaction Company then being forwarded to the Lithuanian bank.

In actual practice there ended up being some discussion on setting silver based prices. How should the price be determined as a starting point? One means was some research to look at the price of goods and services in the 1950s before silver coinage had become too valuable not to circulate. Some things went "backwards" by taking the modern price and using the spot price of silver to determine an initial price. The free market took care of the rest.

There was one problem that required a solution from the 1860s. With the smallest denomination silver coin being the dime, it had a value of anywhere from $1.25 in federal currency on up. Using silver based prices, there were items that would cost less than ten cents, and a solution was needed. The current one and five cent coins essentially had no value in a silver based currency system. The answer was fractional paper currency in denominations the same as the coins. Now practically all of the silver coinage could serve as the currency reserve and were not needed for circulation.

Chapter 9

Polyticks

In the liberty movement the term Polyticks had become popular for describing having to interact with government. The origin of the term was obvious, deriving from the Greek – Poly meaning many and ticks as in blood sucking pests.

Toward the end of the school year, one of the children in Freedonia brought home the report of a teacher who had less than kind things to say about George Washington and Thomas Jefferson. This was a subject of discussion at the next militia meeting. Subsequent investigation revealed that in the last two presidential elections, Borden County had two votes for the Green Party.

This issue was brought up to the community leaders in Freedonia. Such sentiments were out of place with the school district values, so an inquiry was made to the school Superintendent and school Board about some personnel choices. Feedback was that it was hard to staff rural school districts. The people tended to be in their 50s and older, or very young in their first teaching jobs, who would move on to larger cities when they could.

The residents of Freedonia had a solution for that problem. One family member had a Texas Teachers Certificate, and the Freedonia community had friends who were teachers and would gladly move to Borden County. It so happened that one of the community members had a father who was retired as a school superintendent and was available if such difficulties persisted. At the end of the school year, three contracts of school district employees were not renewed. The Green Party lost its supporters in Borden County, and the militia increased the number of its members residing in Borden County by one.

In the next school board election, three of the seven seats were occupied by residents of Freedonia. The message was sent that the citizens expected their schools to teach the skills required of a citizen in a republican form of government. Among that curriculum is an appreciation for the principles upon which the United States and Texas was founded. The American and Texas Revolutions were extraordinary occurrences, which resulted in citizens who had the opportunity to have a degree of liberty and prosperity unparalleled in the history of mankind.

The sheriff was a bonus. A number of west Texas counties had either a part time or full time sheriffs of the old school. He considered his job to be handling the disputes that could not be worked out in any other way and protection of the people from any evil doer that happened by. He drove a pickup, wore a straw cowboy hat, checked shirt, blue jeans and cowboy boots. The badge and 1911 model handgun completed the ensemble. Sheriff Connors was such a man in his late 50s. He was very easy going because nothing happened in Borden County as nothing was going to happen in Borden County. If something did happen in Borden County, the odds were that it was going to be already over by the time Sheriff Connors arrived. He and Roberts took an instant liking to each other. The sheriff and friends were routinely invited to come out to the ammunition factory for shooting samples of new production ammunition lots for quality control purposes.

The citizens of Freedonia ensured that Sheriff Connors remained in office.

The size of Freedonia meant that it would end up electing one of the county commissioners, and Ed McMasters was selected for this task. Other than expecting to be left alone, Freedonia didn't want anything from the county. And the county didn't spend more money than previously as a result of Freedonia and the influx of population. That helped to keep relations between the new and previous residents cordial. It also helped that more people in the county meant some more business for the stores in Gail.

So far, the school issue had been the only rough spot between the two groups. It was made easier to handle by the thinking of the old timers that there wasn't any way to fight what they were told had been state requirements. The fact that community standards could be enforced in the schools helped to smooth over any hard feelings. It helped in understanding why the people of Freedonia were there. They too, liked Texas the way it used to be. The militia gained a few new members.

The district judge, district attorney, and county attorney, were all residents in Snyder from neighboring Scurry County. That was a mixed bag. In the future the Freedonians would have to look at how that played out. As the legal jobs were part timers, you wondered how much influence you had, but the job may be a substantial part of a rural lawyer's income that he did not want to lose. A sensitive point would be the district judge. When the squeeze was on, would he give in or stand with the citizens. There was not yet enough Freedonia population to ensure a positive impact on that election. However, the leading citizens of Freedonia made it a point to "happen" to be at some of the same places at the same time the judge was, in order to start to make themselves known.

As elections were happening soon, both the DA and District Judge were curious to find out about the residents of Freedonia. There were rumblings about candidates being run for the offices, and both wanted to find out if the citizens of Freedonia were going to cause a problem, Both were told that it came down to one thing. Any government official from the President of the United States to dog catcher was expected to be subject to the law in the same manner as any other citizen. Any public official who thought or acted in such as way as to indicate that government officials were exempt form any law would be replaced with someone that has a view toward government officials being subject to the same laws everyone else was expected to obey.

The other county office requiring attention was emergency management. The citizens of Freedonia would work to get one of their own in this position, as it was a major interface with the state government, and information about Borden County needed to be scrutinized before it went to the state government in Austin.

The good news was that it turned out that many of the residents had similar views as the newer residents. It just took some re-enforcement of previously held beliefs to provide some more courage. That helped to cement the relationships between the residents of Freedonia and the rest of the county.

The operation in Freedonia gave Free Texas a solid base of operations and now a functional model of what Free Texas thought was the future of Texas. The program was now more than theoretical, there was an operational entity that could be used as an example. There was evidence as to what worked and what did not.

This was helpful in presenting the Free Texas marketing messaging and future political action, which could now focus on members of the state legislature and assisting county directors in moving their counties toward the working model.

Rampaging Elephants was in on the plan as well. Listeners were kept up to date with progress reports and interviews with several of the residents of Freedonia. It helped to motivate the supporters of Texas independence that some progress could be made without having to elect people to statewide office. Rampaging Elephants now increased its coverage of local Tea Party groups. Once these people concluded that the Republican Party could not get the job done, they would be looking for alternatives. Rampaging Elephants and Free Texas would be ready with that alternative.

Roberts set about creating as much of an auxiliary operation as he could via Free Texas. There was important information that he would need to know. In the Army, this information would be referred to as Priority Intelligence Requirements. In the real world, it was a request to call me if you hear about a large number of vehicles with government license plates traveling together, anything involving the Department of Homeland Security, or something the government is doing that seems odd. Over time, he hoped to build a better intel network, but for now, a journey of a thousand miles again begins with a single step.

Now that there was a community to defend, the Borden County Militia set about incorporating community defense plans into the training regimen. Freedonia was situated so that there was a single gravel road to and from town joining the paved Farm to Market road that connected to Highway 180. As the major highway in the county, it ran to Gail, the county seat where the courthouse, jail, and sheriff's office were located. Roberts intended that to be the main area of operations, being as they controlled the land around Fredonia, and the gravel road, a defensive plan, with fighting positions and obstacles could be prepared. They would only be able to execute any plan involving the gravel road intersection to Gail during a crisis period.

Attention turned toward the needs for a longer term presence in the county and permanent operations within the community. This required gaining control of the county appraisal district. Texas had become hooked on property taxes as the means of funding the public schools and county operations. One of the principles of the Free Texas movement was to eliminate property taxes in favor of funding government by taxes on economic activity. Anyone in the county who got annoyed with the activities in Freedonia could try and strangle the operation by greatly increasing the property valuation.

Thus, the appraisal district and tax assessor – collector needed to be controlled by Freedonians. This was important for yet another reason. In a small county such a Borden, the tax assessor – collector also conducts voter registration. Vital to the success of the project was to maximize the voting rolls of Freedonia. Texas is fairly liberal in establishing residence for voting. After becoming a Texas resident, one can establish voting residence almost anywhere one wishes – there are practically no restrictions. A number of the residence lots were owned by Free Texas supporters who had to work in more populated cities. However, they could establish residence in Freedonia, and move voter registration there. As long as they controlled the office that processed the registrations, there would be no difficulties with those "weekend residents" voting in Borden County.

Free Texas had a couple of attorneys that became members. This was most useful, for several reasons. It assisted in the ability of Free Texas to engage in "lawfare" being the ability to use the legal system to accomplish its political objectives, or prevent opponents from using the legal system for their purposes. This had become a major component of struggle in the public arena. More importantly for the purposes of the Freedonians, there was the possibility of mounting a "legitimate" challenge to the District Attorney or District Judge if those two became a problem. In rural Texas, both jobs were easy work for an attorney, as there might be one trial a year in the county, and you got paid even if nothing happened.

Therefore, it was important to let both attorneys become aware of the fact, that if they became a problem, an effort would be undertaken to replace them. Surely it would be easier on all concerned to keep things as they were, assuming the elected officials were responsive to the standards of the community. Both wanted the message made a bit more explicit. It was simple they were told, in any conflict between Texans and the federal government, there would be no free pass for feds – they would be held to the same standards as any other citizen in their actions. No free pass for any federal agent violating a Texas state law, prosecutions would be expected to occur. Both officials wondered what that was about, but as yet there was no issue, so no problem.

The town of Freedonia was developing nicely. As this was a long term project set up by individuals, there was no pressure to maximize immediate returns on investment as would be the case on a Wall Street financed operation. The investors had objectives in addition to earning a decent return. The Town square was basically a park with the water tower and pump house. There was one row of storefronts, which housed the economic activity of the town. Four of the five storefronts were occupied. The fifth was vacant so that there would be an immediate place for someone who wanted to found the next business in Fredonia. The intention was that after all five storefronts got occupied, the free market would take it from there. There was room for three more sets of storefronts around the town square.

One of the storefronts housed the general store. Buying goods in town saved some gas money, so that trips to Lubbock for major purchases only had to be made once or twice a month. This store also provided a market for locally grown produce. This gave residents the option (most were "preppers") of concentrating on one or few crops on their tracts of land, or even concentrating on other activities, thus being assured that crops were being grown in the area and there was access to the resulting harvest.

Another storefront held the technology company. It had built out a server room, brought in high speed bandwidth to the community, and had a conference room for rent in addition to a WiFi public network. Hosting servers for Free Texas minded businesses, renting the conference room (Free Texas used it frequently so board members could virtually attend county meetings), and being the local ISP paid the bills.

The Freedonia Transaction Company occupied a storefront. The layout was a throwback to a 19th Century western bank. On entering, to the right, one saw a counter with three teller windows, on the left was a half wall high office where account business could be conducted, and then the safe room, and manager's office in the rear behind a door that separated off the public part of the establishment. There was one laptop computer and printer present, and depending on the need, moved from the teller counter to the office.

The fourth of the occupied storefronts was the café. As of yet, Freedonia would not have been large enough to make such an operation profitable. However the amount of deliveries and construction ensured that there would be some number of non residents present in town at midday or into the late afternoon. That supplied enough business to keep the café operating until the population of the town could support it.

Visitors noticed two unusual things about Freedonia. Almost every adult had a habit of going about armed. Various handguns were openly carried, also the women, including the waitresses at the café. Some of the men also carried rifles, predominately ARs. The other unusual aspect of Freedonia is that businesses in town also had two prices listed for every item. One price was labeled in TXD and the other FRN. It seemed that only the visitors used US currency and paid the higher FRN price. Any inquiry about this pricing would produce an explication on the benefits of sound money and the evils of a fiat currency. The visitor would then be asked to consider that the TXD price is the same as would have been paid in 1950 as a matter for consideration.

Things were going well in Freedonia. Activities subject to sales tax were done in the town limits, so that Freedonia would get the 2% revenue. People did the town functions in their spare time, pending town growth to possibly creating a part time clerk job. Funding priorities were the water system, then starting work on an electrical generating capability, and when that was operating, maybe paving some streets. The militia would take on the volunteer firefighting role. Nothing more needed to be done.

Free Texas, and in many ways Rampaging Elephants now had a means to send the message that the US government was destroying the country, and Texas was the ark that could save the parts of the country worth saving. The message tended to resonate more with social conservatives. No matter what they tried to do, the message was just not reaching enough people.

The Free Texas board was discussing this problem one evening at the technology company after a county meeting. Roberts was more philosophical. "We have built the pilot project and it is successful. We are sending the message that the lifeboat is here and there is room. Some people think long term and get the message. Others have to be hit on the head with it like a mule. Some will never get it. What we are doing here will grow and start to annoy somebody in power so much that he won't be able to tolerate that so many people are living lives of freedom outside of his control. We have insulated ourselves from the pending economic disaster as best as individuals can. When that happens, that will provide the spark that ignites the powder keg of liberty.

We just have to wait for that day."

Chapter 10

No Warrants Shall Issue

The IRS likes tax evasion cases. They are a no way to lose situation for the IRS. It gives the agency a way to say to the public, that you can rest assured that we go after fat cats and even average citizens that refuse to pay their fair share of taxes. Therefore, you should go ahead and pay knowing that nobody can get over on us. While a majority of people have a rather simple and straightforward tax situation the message worked. Increasingly, the only people that met that definition became the percentage of the population on public assistance. By the 21st Century, it had reached the point where a substantial part of the population no longer paid income tax. Meanwhile, the tax system had become increasingly complex for the slight majority of the population that paid taxes to the extent that they had to hire companies to figure out their taxes. Fact was, the tax system had reached the point to which almost no one could accurately predict how much in taxes they would owe in the coming year.

Such ambiguity worked to the advantage of the IRS. Anyone could be audited for any reason, additional taxes and penalties imposed, and the taxpayer would bear the burden of proof to the IRS that the taxpayer was correct. Roberts had experienced this every year while working overseas. The IRS would audit his return based on the revenue code and send a bill for additional taxes and penalties. The IRS routinely ignored the provisions of tax treaties with other countries, which would determine what income was taxable in which country, and the amount of overseas income excluded from US taxation. Roberts became convinced that he knew international taxation better than the IRS did. Given the caliber of employee that Roberts dealt with at the IRS, he considered that a not particularly bold statement.

Roberts dealt with the problem every year by reminding the IRS that tax treaty provisions over ride anything in the Internal Revenue Code, and his taxes were prepared according to Department of the Treasury implementing instructions for his country of residence, and just to make sure there was no doubt about his intentions, he had already filed a case in US Tax Court in order to get a legally binding precedent set. This usually had the desired effect. The government hates having its own rules used against it, and would cave in, rather than argue the point in the Tax Court. The amount contested was small, but a legally binding precedent could be used by the major tax payers overseas. The IRS could not afford the risk of a loss in Tax Court. Although there was that one year when he got a bill for $68 as the additional interest on the tax that he did not owe the government.

Roberts liked to quote a Department of the Treasury publication "Tax avoidance is perfectly legal and encouraged by the IRS, but tax evasion is against the law." He had become all about tax avoidance, but the IRS had gotten to the point that it could no longer tell the difference, and more menacingly, no desire to do so. Conflict was going to be inevitable. Certain patterns had come to the attention of the IRS office in Austin relating to income reported by almost all of the residents of the community of Freedonia. They all reported miscellaneous income on Form 1099, and at a level below a threshold that yielded taxable income. Yet, IRS demographic data concluded that these people had to have hundreds of thousands of dollars in assets and a greater income than reported to support that degree of wealth.

This warranted further investigation. After making the rounds in the Austin regional center of the Internal Revenue Service, a warrant was obtained from a Federal Judge to seize the records, computers, and any other assets from the Freedonia Transaction Company for the purpose of obtaining evidence of tax evasion, money laundering, and any other evidence or persons to be found on the premises. A deployment of the Special Response Team was authorized to serve the warrant. Whatever it was those people in Freedonia were doing to evade paying their fair share of taxes was soon coming to an end.

It was going to be over three hours of drive time to Borden County, so the SRT checked out three white SUVs with tinted glass for their G-rides. There was plenty of room for the eight of them, the evidence that would be returned and a couple of prisoners sure to be rounded up. Freedonia had not yet made any of the maps, but Google Earth showed a two gravel street Podunkville. The address for the Freedonia Transaction Company was not clear, as the Transaction Company used a Post Office box in Gail, and the registered corporate agent was not even in the same county, but a lawyer in Austin. It couldn't be hard to find it once they got there.

The team left at 8:30 the next morning. This would be an easy if long day, and the best part of it being that they would get overtime due to the late hour of their return. The agents decided to have lunch in Abilene as it was the last city of any size before heading into the sticks. From I-20 west, they headed north on US 84. A quick stop was made in Snyder for fuel and to kit up for the raid.

Highway US 180 took then the rest of the way to the turn off to Freedonia.

As the three SUVs approached Freedonia, the agents could see the layout of the town. There was a town square with a water tower and a small building, probably the pump house. On the west side of the square was a street running north south with a row of storefronts on the west side of the street facing east. One of those storefronts had to be the Freedonia Transaction Company. The three SUVs turned north and as they passed by each storefront, all they saw was a number – 100, 102, 104, 106, and 108 on the north storefront. The radio chatter started.

"Which one is it?"

"Don't know."

"Pull around back, we'll sort it out from there."

Not much happens day to day in a small town in Texas. The effect of having three white SUVs with tinted windows pull into town was about the same as a troop of naked boy scouts marching through a village of cannibals.

Beth Dunwoody had seen the convoy pass by the front window and immediately knew what it meant. She hit the alarm which sent the text to Roberts' phone. She immediately dialed Roberts number, which went straight to voice mail. The USB drive for the day, and all the cash present was locked in the safe. She waited for the raid to start.

Roberts was at the ammunition plant when the text message arrived. He told the militia members there to stop work, grab weapons and assemble at the water tower. On the way to the water tower, Roberts called as many militia members as he thought were in the area, with the same message and to spread the word. Lastly, he called Sheriff Connors with the news that he had gotten an alarm from the Transaction Company and suspected something was happening. When he got to the voice mail from Beth, his suspicions were confirmed.

Some 16 of the militia members were at the water tower when Roberts arrived. He gave them the briefing that three white SUVs were spotted in town by the storefronts and they would as stealthily as possible make their way behind the storefronts and check out the area. The men moved toward the southwest, using whatever obstructions possible to aid in masking their movement.

The three SUVs turned west at the intersection, and then south behind the storefronts and stopped. The eight agents got out and conferred. Two agents would stay behind to cover the back doors, while the other six walked the rest of the way south and turned east to check the storefronts. The first was the general store. The second was the technology company. The manager, on the possibility that the raid was on the servers of technology company or its clients, had set the various locks on the steel door to the server room and hidden the key to the mechanical lock.

The third storefront was the Freedonia Transaction Company. The agents had been deprived of the joy of breaking down the door by having to search for the correct location. The agents were met by Beth Dunwoody in the lobby.

"Who are you and what do you want?" Beth asked.

"We are special agents of the Internal Revenue Service here to execute a warrant in regards to tax evasion. You are under arrest." the lead agent told her.

"Get out of here. You are trespassing." was Beth's response.

Two agents grabbed Dunwoody, and were then were startled to see the holstered Glock at Dunwoody's side. The agents handcuffed her.

"Search her" the lead agent commanded.

One of the two female agents on the raid then moved toward Dunwoody.

"Just my luck to get the lesbo." was Dunwoody's reaction.

In addition to the Glock, the only thing found on Dunwoody was a key. "That has to be the key to the back door, let our people in." the lead agent decided.

As soon as the Freedonia Transaction Company had been identified, the agents in the back had wanted to enter from the back to at least try to have some element of surprise on anyone who had been in the back of the building. The door had been designed to prevent unauthorized entry from outside and had done its job. The two agents in the back came in as the search was underway. Agents liked to create as much of an inconvenience to the subject of a warrant as possible, by dumping out bookcases and taking drawers out of furniture and dumping out the contents to be stepped on and defaced.

The search of the Freedonia Transaction Company was most unsatisfying. The agents had found one branch manager, one

Glock handgun, a key, a laptop computer and a safe. Every drawer was empty. The agents took Dunwoody back to the safe and four of the agents went out the back to bring the vehicles around front.

The head agent looked at Dunwoody. "Open it."

"No" she replied.

"Open it or else …" one of the agents tried to sound menacing.

"Or else what, you're going to shoot me?" Dunwoody had no fear.

"We'll blow it open!" the agent retorted.

"To blow that safe open, you will end up leveling the town in the process." Dunwoody informed the agent.

The four agents inside heard an excited voice on the radio. "Our vehicles are gone!"

"What do you mean gone?" the lead agent said into his radio.

There was no reply. Beth Dunwoody smiled. The Cavalry had arrived.

The militiamen had arrived at the back of the storefronts in time to see the two agents in the back enter the rear door to the Transaction Company. Roberts motioned and said "Let's go." They approached the SUVs. The agents had left them running with keys in the ignition. That was now a law enforcement standard practice as getting back into a sweltering vehicle while wearing body armor was pure misery.

"You three, drive these things over behind the water tower and come back. Everybody else stack up on the back wall and wait. You two work your away around to watch the front and see if anybody goes out that way." directed Roberts.

One of the militiamen reported back. "Boss, at the café, they said six went in the front door."

Roberts took in the information. "OK, that means for sure eight, could be as many as twelve."

They waited a few minutes, then the door eased open and four agents came out into the sunlight. In the brightness it took them a second to realize the SUVs had disappeared and call back inside. By the time the report of the missing SUVs had been made, each agent felt multiple gun barrels against the body in places not protected by body armor.

Roberts addressed the agents. "Don't say another word."

The agents were relieved of radios and weapons, cuffed and taken to the SUVs behind the water tower.

"Go in or wait?" Roberts was asked.

"Let's see if they send a search party. We have time to wait for an opportunity to peel off some more of them." Roberts decided.

Inside the Freedonia Transaction Company, things were not going according to plan, but then nothing had gone according to plan since arriving in town. The branch manager was totally uncooperative. Branch managers always cooperated because the bank could lose its charter and face millions of dollars in fines if the IRS or Comptroller of the Currency detected any deceit. This woman was impervious to any threat.

One of the agents remarked, "This whole thing has been like a spaghetti western. Next thing we are going to see is the sheriff riding in on a horse."

The head agent decided to call Austin for guidance on what to do about the safe. If they left it unsecured, evidence would be lost. Otherwise they would probably have to sit in place a wait for FBI specialists to arrive to open the safe. He needed to know if they were going to leave or stay.

"You two go see what is holding up those jokers with our G-rides. This is only a two street town and none of these yahoos would be dumb enough to steal a government vehicle. Bring them around front so we can watch them if we are going to be staying here a while." The head agent was getting irritated.

The rear door of the Transaction Company opened, and the agent was surprised when the door seemed to heave open on its own, causing her to lose her balance. The other agent was also taken by surprise when a half dozen rifle barrels were jabbed at him and another half dozen hands pulled him out of the doorway.

"Don't say a word." Roberts told the agents.

The agents were disarmed, radios confiscated, and then were cuffed. Two militiamen were directed to take the agents to the collection point with the other four agents.

"We're going in." Roberts told the others remaining. "If they have not figured out something is up by now, they will shortly. You two to the safe room and teller counter as the base of fire team, everybody else follow me."

The layout of the Transaction Company facilitated this maneuver. The rear door was to a central hall which had the security door at the other end leading to the public area of the company, which closes automatically. Fortunately, the agents had not propped it open as they searched the building. In reality, the security door was more for show, and there was another door from the client cubicle to the manager's office, which should be open, as well as all of the other doors, if search procedure had been followed. This would facilitate the militiamen getting into position to deal with the remaining agents.

The two on the base of fire team members made it though the open door from the hall to the safe room, and found the door to the teller area open. They crouched down low, and started to creep into the teller area. Roberts and the others went into the manager's office, and got into the crouch to make it through the open door into the cubicle. Reflection in the windows showed Dunwoody and two agents present in the public area.

Sheriff Connors got Roberts call relayed to him and told Roberts that he would be on the way to Freedonia, it would take him some 15 to 20 minutes to get there. As Connors arrived in Freedonia, he saw the three white SUVs parked by the water tower and headed directly for them. When he arrived at the water tower, there were four IRS agents and four militiamen holding them prisoner, The militiamen briefed Connors on what had happened. The agents told Connors to release them and arrest the militiamen for interfering with a federal investigation. Connors told everyone, "You fellers just wait right here, and I'll be back."

As Sheriff Connors drove around the square toward the Freedonia Transaction Company, he saw two more cuffed agents being led to the SUVs by two militiamen. His pickup pulled into the front of the Freedonia Transaction Company.

The sound of the pickup pulling into the front of the building got the attention of the two agents holding Dunwoody. The agents also noticed that a crowd had gathered in front of the building consisting of a dozen people, all armed. The driver of the pickup was a man in his late 50s wearing a straw cowboy hat. As the door of the pickup opened, they noticed the cowboy boots and starched blue jeans. Closing the door of the pickup revealed the man was wearing a checked shirt, holstered 1911 pistol, and a five pointed star badge pinned to the shirt.

"'Scuse me folks, I need to see what's going on in there." said Sheriff Connors to the assembled crowd.

The crowd parted, and Sheriff Connors made his way to the door. He opened the door to the Company and addressed the two agents. "I'm Sheriff Connors. Who are you and state your purpose here."

"We're special agents of the Internal Revenue Service here to execute a warrant." replied the head agent.

"Let me see it." Sheriff Connors ordered the head agent.

Connors was handed the warrant and he gave it a quick read. "This isn't a warrant. It's a fishing license. I can't believe that any honest judge signed it."

"We're not interested in your opinion. We are executing this warrant." the head agent told Connors.

"Not in this county. Place your weapons on the table." commanded Connors.

Roberts yelled out "Rise!" and ten ARs were pointed at the two agents by the militiamen. "I suggest you do what the Sheriff said."

The agents slowly placed their weapons on the table. Handcuffs were removed from Dunwoody, and placed on the two agents. Dunwoody told Connors what had happened.

Connors addressed the two agents, "You are under arrest for Official Oppression, theft, criminal trespass, and possibly other charges. I already have the other six of you in the bag. Roberts, can I use some of your men to take these suspects to jail? May I take the laptop, Glock and key as evidence?"

"You got it." was Roberts response. Two militiamen took the agents to the water tower where the others were being held.

Roberts walked with Connors back the sheriff's truck. Connors addressed Roberts "You know Roberts, after seeing the SUVs by the water tower, the four you already had there, and the two on the way, I half expected to arrive and see that you already had the rest of them hog-tied on the floor. It is one thing to have people expect the sheriff to protect them from an over reaching government. It is something else entirely to have people who expect the sheriff to help them protect themselves."

This confirmed that Roberts' confidence in Sheriff Connors was well founded.

Chapter 11

The Right to Trial by Jury

The Department of the Treasury found it incredible that the District Attorney of Borden County, Texas was actually going to prosecute eight IRS agents arrested by the sheriff, and that a District Court in Texas was going to hear the case. The IRS decided that the Department of Justice needed to get on this before other people elsewhere got ideas.

Ordinarily there would be no issue presented here. If some local official caused a problem, going to federal court rapidly put the local troublemaker in his place. This was looking to be different as the whole state legal system seemed to be willing to ignore a federal judge. What would happen when the US Marshals appeared with a federal court order was the unknown.

The sheriff of Borden County was obviously out of control. He had ignored a search warrant signed by a US judge and arrested eight IRS agents charging them with several state crimes, including Texas Penal Code Section 37.03 Aggravated Perjury, Texas Penal Code Section 22.02 Aggravated Assault, Texas Penal Code Section 20.02 Unlawful Restraint, Texas Penal Code Section 29.03 Aggravated Robbery, Texas Penal Code Section 71.02 Engaging in Organized Criminal Activity, Texas Penal Code Section 39.03 Official Oppression, Texas Penal Code Section 31.03 Theft, and

Texas Penal Code Section 30.05 Criminal Trespass while in possession of a deadly weapon.

Bail for the eight agents was denied as they had no connections to Borden County and were considered a flight risk. The Grand Jury returned indictments on all charges. The County Attorney of Borden County went to the Western District US Court in Texas and filed a RICO case against three sport utility vehicles, eight Colt M4 Carbines, eight handguns, eight radios, some 1680 rounds of ammunition, and other assorted items for civil asset forfeiture.

As is always the case when the United States Government is a defendant in a legal action, the government employees are represented by the United States Department of Justice. The lawyer appointed to the case requested a meeting with the District Attorney. The meeting did not go well. The DoJ lawyer told the DA that the agents were acting under the authority of the US Government and they were therefore exempt from state law. The DA replied that would only be correct if the warrant was valid – the DA considered it unconstitutionally vague, and therefore the agents were not operating under proper authority.

The DoJ lawyer got annoyed, "Let's go off the record."

"OK" replied the District Attorney.

"Why are you doing this, you know we are going to win in court?" the DoJ lawyer asked.

"I have a community that wants those guys prosecuted and they are mad at me that less than half the charges are felonies. They would prefer the death penalty." said the DA.

"You know the case law, they are going to get acquitted." The DoJ lawyer said.

"Maybe at the appellate level, but your clients are poison to any elected judge in the State of Texas. What is it you guys always say about a questionable case – let the court sort it out?" the DA was not going to give in.

"What if we get a federal court order for release?" continued the DoJ lawyer.

"I'd guess the judge feels the same way I do, and in any case you would have to serve that order on an uncooperative sheriff who had widespread public support." replied the DA.

"You're really going to prosecute?" the DoJ lawyer was perplexed that a state official would waste the effort.

"Ever hear of those polls and surveys where a bunch of people say the federal government is the biggest threat to liberty in the US? If they had done that survey in my district, the number would be closer to 85%. You can start planning the appeal now. I'm not going to be the DA that loses reelection by being too cozy with the Feds." summed up the DA.

That ended the conversation, and the attorney reported back to the DoJ, that the prosecution was not stoppable. A call was made to the FBI, and a public official corruption case was opened relating to Borden County, Texas. To have agents of the US Government to be tried by a court in Texas for actions taken on duty was intolerable, and would not be permitted. A Department of Justice Joint Task Force was established to deal with Borden County.

Special Agent Douglas Gregory was appointed as the Special Agent in Charge (SAC) of the Joint Task Force by the Director, with Jack Gallagher as his assistant (ASAC). Gregory was a star at the Bureau while Gallagher was on his way out. Gallagher was placed on the JTF because he was ex Army and had been an infantry officer. He also got along well with many of the agents. Gregory was on his way to the Senior Executive Service for aggressively highlighting the role of federal law enforcement on his prior assignments. The two men took an instant dislike to each other. They were at opposite ends of the profile of FBI agents over the past 30 years.

The FBI would provide the bulk of the manpower, as it was the largest federal law enforcement agency. Senior DoJ counsel was responsible for getting the court order mandating the release of the IRS agents, and other agencies had interest in the JTF, and more especially the funding that this activity could provide and prestige to the parent agencies possibly at the expense of the FBI. ATF was interested in the rumored ammunition production operation in the county, and devoted 24 agents to the JTF. DEA contributed 18 agents, not that there was any suspicion of illegal drug activity, but who knows what might show up.

Based on information provided by the IRS agents, it was estimated that the tea bagger militia group in Borden County numbered some 24 individuals. The IRS agents never saw more than 14, but it was a probability that there were some more militia members, and based on experience with investigating other militias, groups never got much larger than two dozen or so individuals before internal dissention would cause a break up of the group. Law enforcement wanted a good 10 to 1 force ratio, so this put the strength of the JTF at 240. Even that number was going to be tough to make. Agents would have to be brought in from all over north Texas and neighboring states. As Gallagher pointed out, it was putting more people on the ground than could be effectively controlled. The JTF was much larger than an Army infantry company.

Gallagher didn't think much of the plan at all. A massive convoy of agents was going to descend on Freedonia, and agents would sweep through town, building by building and house by house, rounding up militia members. Then the ATF would raid the ammunition operation, and the remaining FBI agents would head for Gail to free the IRS agents, as the sheriff would than be isolated from any support. The whole thing was going to be mass confusion and very likely that shots would be fired in the process. Even if only half of the 24 resisted, the operation could easily end up with over 50 people, both suspects and agents shot.

In fact, Gallagher thought the whole operation stank, from the bullshit warrants, to the not letting the legal process work its way, to the assumption that the militia would roll over as individuals. OK, maybe the IRS agents got surprised, but to do that, the militia had to show some degree of courage to confront them. That was something the FBI had yet to see in a militia. If the FBI ever ran across a militia prepared to fight and was even halfway competent about it, the luck the FBI had so far could easily run out. And the plan itself seemed more like a search and destroy from back in the days of the Vietnam War. It was all too ambitious.

Gregory seemed unconcerned. This would be the biggest FBI operation ever against the militia movement and it had the personal attention of the Director. Additionally, Gregory had additional assets allocated to the operation which he could not share with Gallagher. "Jack, this is going to make my career and be the capstone of yours. The Director will thank us personally and publicly for this."

"Doug, nobody has shown this degree of defiance to federal authority before. It is potentially the whole county." Gallagher told Gregory.

"That is why we have to show the tea baggers that they can't get away with it." Gregory insisted.

That statement confirmed a suspicion in Gallagher's mind. This really wasn't a law enforcement operation. This was to demonstrate to the political opponents of the administration the willingness and the ability of the US government to crush its enemies. People in Washington were playing with fire. And fire usually burns something.

The plan was for a five day operation. On the first day, personnel assembled in Dallas and Lubbock. On the second day, the Dallas team traveled to Lubbock and gave the final briefing to the assembled JTF that would make the raid. Day three was the raid itself and transfer of prisoners and material to Lubbock. Day four was the return of the Dallas team to Dallas, and Gregory flies to Washington for the press conference with the Director. On day five, the Dallas team returned agents to home stations.

Gallagher had even more misgivings on Day 1 as the Dallas team assembled. Part of the Dallas Team was the FBI Hostage Rescue Team (HRT). Part of this outfit was the FBI's snipers. They apparently had orders with which Gallagher was not familiar. On this mission the HRT reported directly to Gregory. Gallagher also heard one of the DEA agents tell Gregory they had brought the special package – something else was afoot. And even more shocking was the arrival of an ABC reporter and cameraman "cleared by the Director", who were going to be along on the raid.

Gallagher sensed disaster, and some of the older agents confided in Gallagher their unease as well.

The die was cast, and the rest would now be in the hands of fate. Borden County was destined to become famous.

The Borden County jail housed eight prisoners and was full. No one in living memory could recall when the jail had so many prisoners. The prisoners took a disproportionate amount of Sheriff Connor's time, which as he remarked could have been worse, if there had been much for him to do anyway. It now required additional personnel to be at the jail full time, a very rare occurrence. One thing was for certain, it would be a while before the normal routine of life in Borden County returned.

The arrest of the IRS agents did not generate much media attention. What little there was could be found in the conservative press and specialized outlets such as Rampaging Elephants, which had done an extensive interview with Sheriff Connors. Free Texas certainly made use of the events in Borden County. It demonstrated that this was just one more example of federal government overreach. But this was different. Now the people of Texas were fighting back. Even more importantly, the people of Texas were fighting back successfully. It made a great story for the movement. The story of the IRS raid did bring some attention to Freedonia in the conservative media where there was a debate on whether or not the arrest of the IRS agents was acceptable behavior. There was no doubt about the propriety of the action in the liberty movement. They considered this action long overdue.

Militia training in Borden County took on an increased level of seriousness. Contingency plans for the arrival of uninvited guests were refined. As Roberts told them, events in Borden County had now put everything going on here onto the radar screen of everyone with a stake in the future of the United States and Texas. The days of being a nothing of importance in the middle of nowhere were now coming to an end. The time had come to be weighed by the scales of history, and their efforts had best not come up short. They had to prepare to defend their lives, their fortunes, and their sacred honor.

The day when they would need to do so was sure to come.

Chapter 12

Stand To Horse

As Roberts' cell phone rang, he glanced at the number to see who was calling. It was one of his lookouts in Scurry County. This piqued his interest immediately. "What do you know that's new?" Roberts asked.

The report was one that caused what people in the military refer to as a "this is it" moment. "I saw a bunch of vehicles with US Government license plates heading into Lubbock. There could easily have been over 40 of them traveling on highway 84. That was about 10 minutes ago."

"You have no idea how much I appreciate this." Roberts said.

"After what you guys did to the IRS, I think that I do. Good luck" With that the call ended.

Roberts had two lucky things happen to him with that call. He could anticipate that the raid was going to come from the Lubbock regional office, after agents had started from Dallas earlier in the day. There was a good chance the raid party was going to do its final brief in the Lubbock office, overnight in Lubbock, and head for Borden County early in the morning. He would arrange for one of the sympathizers in Lubbock to do a drive by of motels in town during the evening to confirm or deny this suspicion.

In any case, there was no time to waste. The time to assemble the militia company for the most critical event of its existence had come.

For almost 50 years, any US soldier assigned to US Army Europe, the III Corps, or the XVIII Airborne Corps knew at any time he could be notified with a two word phrase that would initiate a frenzy of activity. In less than four hours, all unit personnel were to assemble, load all unit equipment on vehicles, and be prepared to go to war. Such calls are unforgettable to any who received them. Roberts brought this tradition with him to the Borden County Militia. He called the company second in command (XO).

"Yes sir, what's happening?" the XO asked.

"Lariat Advance this is no drill" Roberts told him.

The call was repeated to the platoon leaders and the company HQ section leaders. One of the section leaders who had been eager to get it on with the feds could not help himself, and replied "Outstanding!" Roberts figured at least one guy was going to show up.

It was already toward the end of the working day, so Roberts headed home to get his gear and to uniform up. While on the way, he gave the sheriff a call.

"Jim Roberts here sheriff. We got word that a 40 plus vehicle convoy of feds was headed for Lubbock. I expect they will be paying us a visit shortly. Have you heard anything?"

"No. You figure they are going to try a jailbreak for their IRS buddies?" Sheriff Connors asked Roberts.

"At a minimum. They may have other objectives as well." Roberts answered.

"Looks like I'm going to be outnumbered if that happens. As Sheriff of Borden County, I am now exercising my authority of the county emergency board under Section 431.112 of the Texas Government Code to order you as commander of the available Texas Military Forces present in the county to parade your unit for the purpose of safeguarding prisoners held by me and to protect the lives and property of the citizens of the State of Texas present in Borden County. That letter will be signed by me and in my desk. Does that give you the authority you need?" Connors said.

"That should do it. They may be bringing a habeas corpus from a federal court." suggested Roberts.

"Don't care. They are charged with state crimes and a state court is going to handle it. When do you think they are going to get here?" Connors was curious to know.

"If they are doing a brief in Lubbock and then heading out, about 3 hours. They may wait for night in order to use night vision, or they may hit at first light. We will be set up either way. From highway 180 to Freedonia is not a good place for people to be for the next 24 hours. If things go well for us, you may have 200 more prisoners and you have no place to keep them" responded Roberts.

"Got it. I'll check with the school district – I'm thinking the football stadium as a prison camp. But, some other idea might strike me in the mean time. Medical?" Connors was going through the possible actions he needed to take.

"I should have a three man medic team and we have some gear and stretchers, but at best it is going to be military medicine, meaning we hope to stabilize, but they will need evacuation pronto. And I'm afraid to tip off the EMS system that we think something is about to happen here." Roberts recommended.

"Agree. I'll work on rounding up some support here on the quiet. Good luck and God bless." Connors ended the conversation.

With the conversation over, Roberts was now home and had parked. Most soldiers have a ritual for dressing and loading the gear in the vehicle for field duty. He got dressed in uniform, repacked the wallet to leave credit cards and other unneeded items behind. Thus, he just had his military ID card, driver's license, and handgun license as Texas did not yet have Constitutional carry. He checked the helmet bag which was the "office" he carried, decided on taking the small backpack with his PVS-14 night vision, a six pack of Cokes, and a couple of MREs which would do for the operation. He decided to bring both the M4 carbine and his M16A4 clone with the Trijicon ACOG in case a longer distance shot was needed. Being Texas, it had low prospects of rain for the next 24 hours and the temperature was not going to get that cold at night, so just the gore-tex parka in the backpack would do.

Roberts decided to make a sandwich and grab some snacks on the way out, double checking that he had everything. On the way to the rally point, he made his next call to one of the Free Texas organizers.

"Hi Jim, what's up?" Ed McMasters asked.

Roberts gave Ed the story. "I think we are about to get raided by the feds. We need to get ready to deal with loads of reporters, because I think big news will result from this. If you still have contact with the Fox channel in Lubbock, you might suggest there will be something newsworthy happening here soon, and I'm willing to have a camera crew along when it happens. They may get some exclusive footage. After profiling Freedonia a couple of months ago, they might like a follow up. And there is one more thing. I need our people in Lubbock to check locally on Highway 84 and the Interstate going south for a convoy of about 40 vehicles with US Government license plates traveling south and get that news back to me. They are in Lubbock now and we need to keep an eye on that."

"OK, where are you going to be, when and where should the Fox crew meet you?" McMasters wanted to know.

Roberts gave him the location of the rally point. "We are meeting there now, so the crew can show up any time, but if they are not there by 0530 in the morning, I think they will miss the action."

"I'll see what I can do, and call you back." Ed replied.

"I'm turning off the phone, so sorry, I need you to deliver the news in person." Roberts told him.

"All right, so what are you going to do?" Ed asked Roberts intentions.

"You'll see when you get here." remarked Roberts

"See you later, bye." Ed hung up the phone.

A few minutes later, Roberts arrived at the rally point. About a dozen men were already there. Roberts started in on the sorting out of the area. "OK first thing is to eat dinner if you have not already. Next we need to hide the vehicles as best we can, even shuttle some vehicles back into Freedonia, bringing the vans and pickups back. We will collect personnel here. As soon as the platoon leaders arrive, I'm going to need them, the commo chief and the supply sergeant. When the XO and First Sergeant get here, they will take over the disposition at this location using the platoon sergeants to sort out who we have and where we have holes in the squads to fill. I'm setting up over by that tree for now. Questions?"

The company had been here before on training, so the troops knew what to do and got to work. Most of those already present were prior service and had grabbed something to eat along the way, More men were arriving, and Roberts handed over the keys to his car to have it moved back. It was a teaching point. Leaders can not issue orders that they do not obey themselves.

Command decisions involve trade offs. The feds could have a drone overhead observing them now. In that case, dispositions would have to be made at the last possible moment, and Roberts would have to let them think that the whole unit could be bagged in the assembly area. They had to be drawn into the engagement area where the company would be able to fight. Or to quote Sun Tzu: The successful commander brings the enemy to the battlefield, he is not brought to it by the enemy. Or, in the more modern Army parlance – gain and maintain both the strategic and tactical initiative.

When the commo chief got there with his equipment, he would know more. Data feeds from drones were not yet encrypted, so if those frequencies were clear, that would be evidence that the feds either didn't think a drone was necessary, or couldn't get one allocated for the mission. He would also have his own tactical drone up. Anything he got from the drone would be a bonus in his view. He was not one of those commanders who could not make a decision unless he had perfect information. He thought that was one of the weaknesses of the modern Army, too much raw data being shoved at commanders that would inflict command paralysis when up against a competent opponent.

More of the men were arriving and platoon leaders were making their way over to Roberts. He asked for preliminary strength reports. So far, about half of the unit had arrived, and about one third were ready for duty. Roberts wanted to give them the operations order while they still had some daylight.

Roberts started in with the order. "OK, here is the situation. A convoy of some 40 vehicles of feds was spotted headed for Lubbock earlier this afternoon, I estimate that to be about 200 agents, and I think they are on their way here to free the IRS guys captured earlier, possibly arrest the sheriff, us, raid the bank where we have our silver, and would not be surprised if the ATF is along to raid the ammo plant. Essentially I think their objective is to stamp out the liberty movement and they are starting here.

The sheriff has activated us according to the Texas Government Code to protect his prisoners from jailbreak, and prevent the violation of the rights of the citizenry. We hope to have the whole company and possibly the help of some volunteers. Not sure what I'll do with the volunteers yet.

Our mission is to stop that raid, and if possible capture the raiders for charges to be filed by the district attorney. If necessary, we will kill those that can not be captured. This mission has enormous political implications for us, Texas, and the United States. Therefore, it is necessary to keep the number of enemy killed to a minimum, consistent with protecting the lives of our own personnel and families.

The operation will be conducted by executing an ambush along the road to Fredonia, where we have prepared the fall away sections of the road. While this will be similar to previous training exercises, the difference is that not all of the enemy will fit in the planned kill zone. Therefore we will have to change the layout from an L shaped ambush, to a large C in order to cover both possible access routes and the primary kill zone. Look at the sand table over here. This string is Highway, 180, this string the Farm to Market road, and this stick is the road to Freedonia.

I want second platoon here, cutting and covering the road to Freedonia as covering the primary kill zone. I want first platoon to tie in with second to Highway 180 and establish an observation post here. Third platoon ties in with second here and extends to the Farm to Market road. We are going to lay out the "dragon's teeth" in that road to create an obstacle on the route to Gail, if that is their primary objective. Sniper teams are assigned to first and third platoons primarily for security, and then engage high value targets – First priority disable communications, second priority disable heavy weapons.

Engagement criteria (A) lead vehicle reaches the prepared cut, second platoon drops the road surface and action starts (B) I have loaded tracer, and when you see tracer go down range (C) You are observed and enemy takes hostile action. (D) Lead vehicle fails to turn to Fredonia and reaches the "dragon's teeth".

Engage using harassing fire. The objective is to create panic that will cause then to fire ammunition carelessly and run them out of ammunition. One to two rounds per man per minute to start should do it. After action starts, first and third platoons need to have the flank squad show movement – low crawl or high crawl is fine – so that they know their escape routes are cut off and draw fire. Nobody runs out from cover.

We will move out of the assembly area here either on order or at 2100 hours, pending intel reports. Once you have set your positions, dig shallow positions, and if you can, suspend tarps over the positions to mask some thermal signature during the night. Assuming we are not hit tonight, stand to will be at 0530.

Make sure everyone has 7 mags of 5.56, full canteen, radio with charged battery, and pick up the field phones and commo wire. The supply sergeant should be here by now or shortly. The supply sergeant also has zip ties for prisoners, they will be split between first and third platoons.

I will locate the company CP here. At stand to and for action I will be at the second platoon, third platoon junction. The XO will be at the CP with the commo chief. We will issue CEOIs before you depart the assembly area, use radio only if you have to move from a wired position. I expect this to be over in 24 hours, so we will resupply either here or by the road down in the kill zone.

I will add any other details at the assembly area before departure. Questions?"

One of the platoon leaders mentioned "That's more guys than we expected to fight."

Roberts replied "If all our guys show up, we should be able to handle over 300. That is what we really trained for – an opposing force as large as three times ours. OK – off you go so you can get in your leader's recon before the sun goes down."

Roberts then walked over to the assembly area, it had been well cleared of vehicles, and the remaining vehicles were dispersed and hid as well as the ground and minimal vegetation allowed. The rest of the command group was there and so was McMasters. It appeared that McMasters had also taken upon himself the role of pizza delivery and some two dozen pizza boxes were now hors de combat. "Good to see you and thanks for the pizza. That's a good morale boost."

"Jim, this must be your lucky day." McMasters told Roberts.

"Good news?" Roberts started to walk McMasters away from the assembly area for a private conversation.

"It seems Lubbock is not that big of a town after all. Your feds were filling up at a truck stop and groups of them having dinner around town. And there is more." McMasters reported.

"Do tell." prompted Roberts.

"Fox news will be here at 10. They want to cover the fight." said McMasters.

"I can't let them broadcast from here and especially not tonight." Roberts had to keep their preparations secret.

"I'm sure they will be disappointed to find that out once they get here. What do you think?" McMasters hinted for a suggestion.

Roberts told his friend "First we will embargo the news crew until after it is over. The footage they will get is the makeup to them, and it will be an exclusive. As for the raid, it means no sooner than midnight would be my guess, which is OK as we will be in position by then. It will take them two hours plus to sort themselves out, get on the road and get here. Night means overtime for 200 agents, so from what I've heard so far, I'd say first light will be the assault so they can be back at the office by mid afternoon. It's the bureaucratic mind at work."

"What do you need me to do?" inquired Ed.

Roberts continued "Several things. First, see if you can help out the sheriff in chasing down some resources he will need – to build a probable detention facility. Second, if we are successful, we will end up in the county seat tomorrow, so we will need hot food and transportation as we start to rotate shifts. Third, we have some no shows. I'm guessing most of them are the pure prepper type, those that really never envisioned a conflict with the feds and Texas sovereignty in the balance. A little family pressure from the neighbors might work here, you know – hey my husband is out there on the line for liberty and why aren't you there?

And most important – if we are successful tomorrow, Borden County is likely to become an international media circus. Free Texas has to be positioned to take advantage of that. This will be an opportunity to get the message out across Texas and the rest of the world. It will be easier on you if we win, but the circus is going to happen no matter how it turns out. They have been able so far to play the IRS agents story as a crazy sheriff thing. This is too big for that. There was not a political movement associated with Bundy Ranch, so the good from that was limited. This is the opportunity for Free Texas to start that ground swell of public opinion support."

"Sounds like our plan is coming together. I hope the people of Texas take advantage of the opportunity they might get." Ed was now optimistic.

"That very well could be." agreed Roberts.

"I've got to say that you seem like natural at this." complimented Ed.

"I come from a background where the highest honor that can be given a citizen is to be entrusted with the lives of your fellow citizens, when the fate of the nation hangs in the balance. After having that degree of responsibility, all other problems in life shrink to insignificance." was the insight Roberts had to give Ed

"Good luck and I hope we can celebrate tomorrow" Ed was heading back to Freedonia.

"May God defend the right." Roberts declared.

The two parted, and Roberts walked back to the assembly area. The sergeants had assembled the company, were finishing the pre combat inspections and preparing to move the squads into position. "Top, how are we on strength?"

"Twelve absent" the First Sergeant reported.

Roberts gave an update to the situation. "Everybody listen up. We are expecting a raid party from about 200 feds. While this is more that we have planned to handle, that is still very much within the capability of a unit our size to deal with if we can achieve surprise, and we have planned properly. If we are able to capture the raiding party, we will score a tremendous political victory to accompany the military victory. The federal government may not be able to recover from the embarrassment and this will be the key to the possibility that we can restore the degree of freedom bequeathed to us by the founders and lead lives of liberty.

The raid may occur as early as midnight, but I expect it at first light.

We have had the advantage of patriotic Texans taking some risk to themselves to provide us with this information, so that we have every prospect of great success. It is now up to us. As long as each of us does as we have trained, we will win. Mere words can not express the importance of the task with which we have been entrusted, but this quote from George Washington comes close:

'The time is now near at hand which must probably determine, whether Americans are to be, Freemen, or Slaves; whether they are to have any property they can call their own; whether their Houses, and Farms, are to be pillaged and destroyed, and they consigned to a State of Wretchedness from which no human efforts will probably deliver them. The fate of unborn Millions will now depend, under God, on the Courage and Conduct of this army. Our cruel and unrelenting Enemy leaves us no choice but a brave resistance, or the most abject submission; that is all we can expect. We have therefore to resolve to conquer or die.'

Let each of us now go and do our duty as God has given us the light to see that duty."

The platoon leaders started to move their units into position. The company was only at 85% strength, and that should be enough.

Fundamentally that was the problem with militias, you never really knew how many people you had for duty until it happened.

At least the core group was there, but those twelve guys would miss the defining moment in the unit's history, and thereby forever separated themselves from those who stood their post and did the duty required of them. At best, they might get a fresh start in another unit. That was the other difference between the regulars and the militia. In the regulars they would be court martialed and have a prison sentence. In a non state sponsored unit, your discipline method was to vote them off the island.

Next, Roberts needed to see the commo chief. "Are we wired in?"

"Almost, sir. We might have TA-1 that went bad and I'll have to replace it with a 312 because we don't have any spare 1s." reported the communications sergeant.

"Been able to monitor any of the known drone feeds or fed frequencies?" Roberts wanted to know.

"Nothing on the drones assuming they are still unencrypted, no noise on the scanner, but you can bet LE will be using encrypted." his commo chief replied.

"I don't have to listen to them, just would like to know if they are around, and we may send them a message in the clear." Roberts provided the commo chief with his intentions.

"I'll let you know if we pick up anything." assured the commo chief.

Now Roberts headed for the XO and First Sergeant, and then the wait for Fox news to show up. The XO and First Sergeant had seven men with them, and Roberts noted that two were from the twelve missing prodigals.

"Sorry to be late sir." Said one of the militiamen.

"The First Sergeant will get you to your platoon leaders." In the regulars there would be a detour along the way for a 'counseling session'. "And have we made some new friends, Top?" Roberts remarked.

"Sir, we have five volunteers who want to do their part" the First Sergeant was happy to inform him.

Roberts addressed the new men. "Let me talk to them while you take the two of ours to their platoons.

Gentlemen, thank you for volunteering. It will be quite a challenge to immediately fit in – this is sort of like showing up in the middle of a movie, but we will do our best to add you to our band of merry men. Any of you prior service?"

Two hands went up.

"Combat arms?" Roberts hoped.

"Infantry" one of the men replied.

"Same here" said another of the five new men.

Roberts took in the good news. "Well that is a bonus. You two will be assigned to First and Third Platoons, the non prior service guys will fill out Second. Second should only have to stay in position and shoot, and we will pair you up with a man who has been in the company for a while. The XO will take you to the Supply Sergeant and see if we have uniforms and field gear for you. Best of luck and I'll see you later."

He waited for the First Sergeant to return. They discussed possible prisoner handling, the contingency plan for if they were discovered before the feds drove into the ambush, and the probability that the sheriff was going to use school facilities for the housing of the captured agents, and by extension, that would become the company's operating base. The XO came back during the conversation and he got the brief as well as the "additional duty" of sitting on the Fox news crew when it showed up, which was expected to be soon. Roberts was then going to troop the line after dealing with the reporters.

He was not even fifteen minutes into scarfing down one of the can Cokes from his six pack, when the Fox news van arrived and was met by the XO, who brought them to Roberts.

The reporters were annoyed at being out here for nothing on the 10 PM news. Roberts knew that would play badly, but suggested the following, get some interview time with McMasters tonight about Free Texas, spend the night at his ranch, and be back in the morning at 5. Roberts would fill them in on what was really happening then. If he told them now, he would require them to spend the night with the militia. He could not let word get out that the militia was having a training exercise, until tomorrow afternoon. At that time the crew would be free to show any footage they took with no restrictions.

Getting that kind of access into one of the larger militias in Texas sealed the deal. Roberts called McMasters with the plan and asked him to pick up the crew. By leaving the van in the assembly area, there was unlikely to be a news leak, and the van driving around the county in the morning was going to give up the game. Roberts also promised them an interview for tomorrow afternoon. He thought that would play to most reporters 'deep throat' fantasies.

After McMasters left with the reporters, Roberts headed for the far right of the company, the security position manned by third platoon.

He visited every position in order that the troops would see him, he got to verify that everybody understood what they were to do in the morning, and lastly to discuss the contingency plan of what to do if they were discovered. The discovered platoon would have to get itself on line to lay down the base of fire, while second platoon would come to support and draw attention from the far platoon which would then try to maneuver and fire into the flank of the attacking force.

That plan needed a well trained company to pull it off, and it would be difficult for his unit to do so if required. However, such a risk to his unit required an opponent that was skilled in light infantry tactics, Roberts was of the opinion that federal law enforcement to date had demonstrated no such proclivities, so the risk was minimal.

He was back at the command post by midnight and told his radio operator he was maybe going to sleep, but have whoever was on duty to wake him at 0445. Roberts didn't expect to get much sleep. He was used to doing 24 hour duty shifts, but after 36 hours people tended to go zombie. He sat by a tree, wound his pack and carbine sling in his arms, so that if someone tried to steal his weapon or pack, the motion would wake him.

As platoon leader of 3rd Platoon, Jeffrey Smith had the task of setting out the "dragon's teeth" and covering the highway on the right flank of the company. He gave his operation order to the platoon sergeant and squad leaders. Much of the order was a mirror of the order the Captain had given him. As approachable as Roberts was on militia duty and off, it was hard to think of Roberts as anything but the Captain.

For the platoon, the concept of operation part of the OPORD, he only told the platoon the general layout of the company, and focused on the actions of the platoon. Smith decided to use the weapons squad as an intact unit, so the highway and flank of the company was covered by the heavier 7.62mm weapons. The other three squads with the 5.56mm weapons would do for harassing the convoy.

The "dragon's teeth" were portable cement blocks about 12 inches square on bottom, about 18 inches tall, and tapering to about 6 by 9 inches on top. They were designed as anti tank obstacles in the 1930s for border defense in Europe prior to World War II. "Dragon's teeth" were designed to rip the bottom out of tanks and immobilize them. The portable ones that the militia were using, were not that strong because they were not fixed in the ground, but wheeled vehicles would have unpleasant consequences if they encountered them. The platoon sergeant was responsible for their emplacement on the road.

Smith had the RTO wire in the phones, and run the platoon line back to the company switchboard. Each of the squad leaders ran his wire back to the platoon command post. In his own experience, he knew the RTO job was a real pain, but that was your last enlisted job before being promoted to sergeant and being made a team leader. He was going to have the platoon sergeant with the weapons squad as an extra set of eyes at the critical point. The stationary defense and wire made his job easier. Without the communications, he would have to do much more walking to get word to the squad leaders.

With the wire run, Smith did the walk of the line, starting on the left to make sure the boundary between third and second platoons was well coordinated and where the limits of fire were for each platoon. Then he did likewise for each of the squads as he worked his way to the right. By the time that was done, there were about six hours left to stand to – that would give him about three hours sleep which would be split with his RTO.

Roberts jerked awake. His watch read 0440. He got up and got ready for the day. Probably the most critical day in his life in years, and maybe for the future of the republic as well. He wanted to be finished shaving before the Fox crew arrived.

All night and even now, his mind was working through the advice from LTG Hal Moore, who commanded 1-7 Cav at the Ia Drang in Vietnam. (1) There is always one thing more I can do that will influence the outcome – what is it? (2) What am I not doing that I should be doing (3) What am I doing that I should not be doing. That was the best description of the responsibilities of a unit leader he had ever seen.

The Fox Crew and McMasters were good to their word, and McMasters appeared with the news crew at two minutes past five. Roberts met them at the van. McMasters drove off. He asked the reporter "Did he spill the beans this morning?"

"You're really expecting an FBI raid and you're going to stop it?" the reporter asked.

112

Roberts affirmed the information. "Stop it or die trying. In any case, I expect that 12 hours from now you are going to be all over the network news with extraordinary footage. Let's get you into position to watch the show while I brief you on what I expect. If all goes well, I will be able to lift the reporting embargo on you by 2PM. If it goes bad for us, the FBI will be lifting the embargo. When this is over, I hope that you will agree that we were less restrictive on you than the Department of Defense would have been."

The crew was in position to cover the company as stand to took effect. The tarps set out during the night were rolled, and the Borden County Militia prepared for action.

Peacetime training is the preparation for war. The professional military devotes a tremendous amount of resources to this task. Private militias have almost no resources with which to work. It relies of the resourcefulness of the individuals, and the experience of the leadership. Ultimately, that experience is the value the prior service combat arms guys bring to the mix. But one thing is the same for militia as for the regulars, a unit going into action for the first time is untested, and one can't know how well the unit will perform beforehand.

History teaches that even well trained regulars can fail in combat. History also teaches that very few militia units performed well in their first combat. Those that did were those with competent commanders, who knew what they were about. Whether or not the Borden County Militia was up to the task was about to be recorded for posterity.

Roberts mused, if I was still commanding a Cav Troop, I'd have the bugler sound "Stand to Horse" for the psychological impact.

Chapter 13

Enemy in Sight

The TA-312 field phone next to Roberts' position buzzed. He answered "Company Commander".

The voice of Roy, the 1st Platoon leader came over the line. "1st Platoon here, OP 11 reports a convoy of at least 30 SUVs, vans, and a couple of busses heading south along the highway. Estimate at least 200 personnel and more coming."

Roberts answered, "OK, hang on and I'll do a net call."

He thought – true to form, no plan survives contact with the enemy. Roberts had initially planned on the raid party to have between 100 and 200 as the unit had conducted its training. Well over 200 meant it was probably a joint team of ATF and FBI. They were trying to minimize their risk after what had happened to the IRS team. They might only get 60% of the raiding force in the kill zone before the ambush was sprung. The good news was no MRAPs, probably due to the distance the convoy had to travel – not that it really mattered. There was a contingency for that, they were committed at this point anyway, and as irregulars, the ambush was one of the things they practiced extensively as the preferred method of attack. We are about to find out if the unit was going to stick to it, hoping that the confidence gained after bagging the IRS guys and the vets distributed throughout the company for leadership would be enough.

Roberts turned the crank on his TA-312 and the company communications chief answered "Switchboard".

"Put out a net call to all platoon leaders and company section chiefs." Roberts ordered.

He heard each of the platoons answer, the sniper squad leader, and the XO, first sergeant, and supply sergeant. The engineer was near Roberts and could overhear the briefing. "We have a few more visitors than we expected, so here is the modification to the plan. The engineer will drop the road as planned, and then go ahead and drop the part by the highway intersection without waiting for all of the vehicles to turn. There are going to be too many of them. So, the snipers will have to disable the vehicles on the highway as first priority, disable vehicles in the kill zone as second priority, and take out commo gear as can. 1st Platoon will have to move 1st squad to seal off the north end of the highway to prevent escape, and 3rd Platoon will need to move your 3rd squad to the south end of the highway to cut off escape. We will still try to capture as many as possible – no intentional kills unless I order or required for survival. Questions?"

There were no questions, and Roberts knew the 2nd Platoon leader didn't like that order – as the guy would rather just whack them all and let the buzzards feast, but this was not the time for that. Roberts also knew that the 2nd Platoon leader was a professional, and would follow his orders. It was one of the things that made this company what it was – militia but still disciplined enough to do what was required because the vets that served as the officers and NCOs were vets and would maintain that discipline.

All of the phone lines dropped except for the communications chief. "I've got radio traffic on a federal LE band, but it is encrypted."

Roberts responded to the news "When the engineer drops the road, break in on them in the clear and demand their surrender. After that, barrage jam them if you can, but I assume they will get word back to Dallas that their plan has something amiss. I'm counting on the three hours reaction time before they get help, so if you get any other SIGINT of feds in the area, that will be important."

The absolute wildest thing about the whole situation was there had been enough warning to put everything in place, down to the Fox news crew set up right behind Roberts getting primo visuals. So far, they had gotten every lucky break. Whether Divine intervention or not, it was appreciated. No matter how it turned out, those guys were going to have one hell of an evening newscast. Roberts got back to business.

Peering over a small berm, Roberts directed his binoculars to the highway. Sure enough, he saw the lead vehicle, a white SUV with the tinted windows so popular with the feds. Instinctively he used the ballistic reticle to calculate the range to target. Not that he was going to call for fire from mortars or artillery, because they did not have such weapons thanks to the US Government. It was habit based on years of experience as an officer of the US Army.

The convoy was moving south down the road, which as is the case with most Texas rural roads, was somewhat elevated with ditches that are two to three feet deep on each side of the road surface. That can make it very hard for a vehicle to maneuver off the roadway should it be necessary to do so. And it is even harder when the ditches have had additional work performed by people not employed by the Texas Department of Transportation and specifically designed to inhibit off road movement. The lead SUV slowed in order to make the right turn onto the road to the west that lead to Freedonia, the ammunition plant, and the other businesses that had been built in the last year. It was the only road in from the highway, and that was by design. Also by design were two hidden bridges on that road, which masked empty space some 10 feet long and just over three feet deep. The ditches along the side of this road were even wider and deeper than on the highway.

After turning, vehicles started to increase speed. The engineer looked at Roberts. Then Roberts nodded, and pointed down with his left index finger. After three cranks on the detonator, 10 feet of roadway some 20 feet in front of the lead SUV dropped into a three foot hole. The driver stomped on the brakes, but the gravel road did not provide traction, and thus the SUV slid into the hole. The forward momentum took the vehicle to the far wall where the bumper hit hard, which deployed the air bags and brought motion to a sudden halt. Roberts found the result very satisfactory – if the US Department of Transportation had not mandated air bags, that crew would be non mission capable for much longer than just a few minutes.

Roberts turned toward the engineer and motioned again with his left hand. Then the second 10 foot section of road, this at the turn off the highway fell. The timing was perfect. The rear of one vehicle fell in, while the bus making the turn off the highway nosed in and partially blocked the south bound lane of the highway. Roberts judged that they got some 60% to 70% of the vehicles in the kill zone, and those on the highway had to decide if they were going to stay with the rest, try to bug out south, or somehow move to the north. As vehicles slid to a stop or collided with each other, time briefly stood still.

Special Agent in Charge Gregory of the Department of Justice Joint Task Force was riding in his SUV which was toward the middle of the convoy. His driver had just made the turn off of the highway on to the road to town and the ammunition plant, and they were accelerating when his driver suddenly hit the brakes. Just as he was about to ask his driver why he was stopping, he heard a crash from behind his SUV. Radios were chattering with talk of the road giving way and not being able to stop in time. What a screw up – he didn't want to bring any of those ATF F-Troop guys with him. This should have been a pure Bureau operation to get the guys who had arrested the IRS team. But the ATF wanted to tag on the ammunition plant and their manufacturing license and hassle the owners about excise taxes due. He had secretly brought along the FBI Hostage Rescue Team, as those guys would have no trouble taking out some Texas militia bubbas. He was sure some idiot agent had caused a smash up.

This was already bad enough as the Director had approved of the ABC news crew coming along to document the arrest of the militia that had captured the IRS team. The story the news was going to get as of now was not going to be career enhancing. He was just about to get out of the SUV to see what the screw up was when he heard over the radio – "This is the commander of the Borden County Militia. Ground your weapons and surrender." He looked at the radio as the voice came on again – "I now demand your surrender for a second time." Just as the SAC was about to grab the radio mike and ask who the hell this was, he saw motion behind him while the voice said – "If you do not surrender, it will be your life." There was now activity up on the road.

Probably every agent in the task force had heard the surrender demand. There could be no doubt about what was happening. The only chance for escape was now. The guys on the gravel road were

118

done for, but the agents on the farm to market road had a chance. The SUV behind the bus edged into the north bound lane to get around the bus and make a dash to the south. As soon as the SUV got even with the bus, a .50 cal round smashed the radiator and lodged in the engine block. Sniper team C was tasked with blocking the escape route to the south, providing covering fire as 3rd Platoon's 3rd squad started to make its way toward the highway. The agents in the SUV decided not to be there in case another round was on the way, and sought cover in the ditch to the east. One agent noticed movement across the farm to market road to his right and opened fire.

Special Agent Angel Ramirez had survived Iraq and Afghanistan, his last tour with the 173rd Airborne Brigade. He did not need anyone to get on the radio to tell him what was happening. He was in the next to last vehicle on the road as he saw the first SUV in the convoy go nose in to the hole. Ramirez screamed "Ambush!" and told the driver to get off the road. The driver was busy braking, when Ramirez grabbed the steering wheel and sent the van across the north bound lane and into the east ditch, where the van stuck. The agents got out and started to move north, Ramirez's combat experience kicked in – "We gotta get out of the ditch, it will be booby trapped!" The agents saw movement across the road to the west and opened fire. They stopped when rounds started to impact five to six feet in front of them. Ramirez dropped his M4, sat down, and put his hands on his helmet. He knew that he was a sitting duck and only still alive because whoever was out there was firing warning shots.

Brandon Jones thought he had the best seat for the show. As a squad leader in the second platoon, his squad covered the road to Freedonia. He had a four man fire team positioned on each side of the road, and would open fire to stop the first vehicle if the road drop failed. Most of the men were excited and did not get much sleep. At stand to, only two of the nine men in the squad were asleep, so it did not take him long to report to his platoon leader that he was ready to fight.

Jones had one of the volunteers assigned to his squad, and he had him fill the spot left by one of men who failed to show. That man had been paired with one of the more experienced militiamen, but Jones, and the new man's team leader would try their best to keep an eye on him. It was good to have the volunteer, but if the squad needed to move and maneuver, the new man would most likely be a liability rather than an asset to him.

Fortunately, he was doing fine and the plan was working. The road surface had given way at the right time and the occupants of the first vehicle had the fight taken out of them. None of the agents dared to move toward them, and they were huddling near the vehicles, thinking of them as providing cover from gunfire. For the most part, they just waited for an agent to try and make a move, and then fire a round nearby or into a vehicle to give the agents a scare. Wild rounds would fly overhead, but for a gunfight, it was starting to get a bit boring.

Sniper teams A and B went to work on the vehicles on the highway. They put several 7.62 rounds into the engine compartments, with the intent to convince the agents that sitting in a vehicle was bad for one's health. Agents were now scrambling out of vehicles and firing. The volume of fire from the agents was increasing dramatically. But the agents were stuck. Every time an agent tried to move, rounds would land three to four feet in front of him. Second Platoon went to work on the vehicles on the road with the same result as on the highway. The agents were pinned down.

The Special Agent on the duty desk of the FBI regional office in Dallas got a strange radio call from Joint Task Force Special Agent in Charge Gregory. "We've been ambushed and you need to get everybody you can out here before they kill us all!"

"WHAT?" was the reply from the office.

Gregory demanded "I said get off your ass and get here! We are being shot to pieces!"

"Where are you? Who is shooting at you? How many of them are there?" the office was seeking more information.

There was no reply. The duty agent tried to call for a few more minutes. Then he looked up Gregory's mobile number and got the out of service area message. He decided to call one of his contacts in ATF. They had people in the Joint Task Force along with the FBI. "Bob – I just got a strange radio call from the SAC on the JTF operation this morning about being under attack and the force getting shot up. I haven't been able to raise him since. I was wondering if you could check with your people on the force, see what was going on and call me back – OK"

ABC reporter Brett Williams was riding with his cameraman in the bus that would be used later to transport the tea bagger militia back to Dallas in federal custody. As the bus turned off Highway 180, there were two distinct pops and then a series of even quicker pops which were not like anything he had heard since the footage taken of a convoy ambush in Iraq. He then saw the bullet holes start to appear in vehicles. He hit the quick dial on his phone to the news desk in Hew York. "It is Brett Williams here, I'm with the FBI team in Texas and we are being ambushed" Then the cell phone call dropped. Redial was unsuccessful. There was no service provider signal.

Tony Garza and Sam Mitchell manned the far left fighting position in first platoon. As soon as the road surface dropped, Tony crawled out a few feet toward the highway. At least one of the occupants in the last vehicle saw movement and cut loose with his M4. The rounds went feet over Tony's head. Tony thought that is just what the Captain said would happen. Roberts had spent several minutes with them last night making sure they knew what he expected them to do. Then Sam moved toward Tony, and that drew more fire. They each fired one round as the other moved, and proceeded to work slowly toward the highway. At first they targeted the vehicles, but then decided to send rounds in the general direction of groups of agents, to keep them from getting any ideas about going somewhere. It was just like training, except for the crack of the sound of rounds passing over them.

Roberts had seen the SUV try to make it around the bus, so he assumed the surrender demand was not going to work at this point. He had loaded up a couple of tracer rounds in the first magazine, and looked through his ACOG to try and spot one of the opposing leaders. He spotted someone with a radio mike in his hand, so he sent the tracers near by to make sure the agent knew that they were taking fire. He was reasonably happy with developments so far. The situation had the company about 300 meters out from the vehicles with the feds pinned down. So far it looked like nobody had been hit, there may be some light crash injuries, and saw no medium weapons or grenade launchers employed by the feds.

There was activity by one of the vans. Some agents were trying to get back to a van, probably to get some gear they intended to use. Roberts figured that had to be stopped. We can't afford some counter sniper activity, when it came down to it there would be no extra risk tolerated to either his men or himself. "All X-ray elements, this is X-ray 47, prevent equipment recovery from the van on the highway, 4th vehicle from the last."

The FBI Hostage Rescue Team was in a bad spot. They (or more accurately, previous members of the Team) had been present at Ruby Ridge and at the Branch Davidian compound in Waco. Those incidents were sore points with the tea bagger movement, and the agents on the Team knew that if given the opportunity, the tea baggers would kill them with relish in revenge. The agents had to get their sniper rifles into action, or they would be dead men. There was no way the average agents, even those who had SWAT training, were going to get the Team out of this situation. The tea baggers were over 300 meters out, and knew that most agents couldn't hit an elephant at 200 meters. The Team had to get back to the van.

Roberts RTO was approaching, saying into the microphone "Standby for X-ray 47 actual." And then he handed the mike to Roberts.

"This is X-ray 47 actual, over." Roberts said.

The sniper team leader had also spotted the activity by the van. "This is X-ray 72, request to take targets by the van down, over."

"Shred the van, knee cap them if you can, then take them down, over." Roberts decided.

"Roger, out." acknowledged the sniper team leader.

The sniper squad leader was from Northern Ireland, had served in the United Kingdom military, and came to the US when the UK confiscated private firearms. The knee cap practice was to inflict crippling injuries on opponents, rather than kill them. It had a certain psychological impact. If the company could, they would destroy whatever was in that van, and failing that, the agents trying to get in the van would be shot and possibly killed.

The .50 cal. and 7.62 shooters now focused on the cargo compartment of the van. The light steel or aluminum of vehicle bodies does not withstand ammunition hits well at all. Gaping holes started to appear in the van, and whenever an agent got near the van, he saw even smaller 5.56 holes start to appear as 3rd Platoon started to enjoy the challenge. At least for now, it was keeping the agents out of the van.

One of the FBI agents could not be deterred. He had slowly worked his way near the van. He sprang up and reached for a rear door handle. That drew a concentration of fire on the rear doors, and the agent felt the hot stings of bullets piercing his hands and lower arms. He dropped and rolled away from the van. The rest of the HRT got the message.

Every small unit action, and this one was no different, consists of tens or hundreds of such actions by individuals and small teams. They are little noted by history, but never forgotten by the participants.

Assistant Special Agent in Charge (ASAC) Jack Gallagher was an oddity in the Bureau, he was an ex infantry officer, and one of the old guys, frequently passed over for promotion and near retirement. He didn't like the SAC, and the feeling was mutual. Gallagher was in the second vehicle from the lead and had spent most of the 30 minutes so far into the action working his way back for the less than half mile that had separated him from the SAC.

He intended to try and convince the SAC to end this. The task force had no way to win, and it was only a matter of time until agents started to get killed, and Gallagher figured they were running out of time fast. He could only move 3 yards at a time before a bullet came uncomfortably close. Then he would have to wait a couple of minutes and try again.

Gallagher finally found the SAC. "Jack, what do you make of it?" Gregory asked.

"We need to end this now." Gallagher told the SAC.

Gregory wasn't sure what Gallagher meant. "You mean attack? Your experience tell you that we can take them? I got in touch with the Dallas office on the radio, and told them we were under attack and they needed to get off their asses. Can we hold out for two hours?" The SAC knew an attack would cost agents, and he might be able to deal with a few losses if that meant rounding up the tea bagger militia. And if it cost more than that, well he had listened to the advice of the infantry guy who got it wrong.

Gallagher had been misunderstood. "No. Get out of here alive before they get bored playing with us and decide to send a message to Washington at our expense."

"Give up? Surrender like that idiot on the radio said?" Gregory's doubts about Gallagher grew.

"Negotiate a withdrawal. As long as nobody has been killed, we have a little leverage." Gallagher tried to reason with Gregory.

"Why would they agree to that?" Gregory wondered.

"Maybe they don't want to kill us. If they did, I think they would have done so already. Maybe they just want to make the point that we can't take them." Gallagher replied.

"I see" The SAC thought maybe Gallagher was on to something. Or, maybe not. Gallagher was never all in on taking down these guys anyway.

A sudden thought then struck Gallagher "It might be even worse. Maybe they are using us as bait, expecting that we have called in for help. They are planning on ambushing the relief column, and then finish us off. As soon as they realize there is no help on the way for us, we will be shot down for sport."

That hit the SAC hard. It had always been a worry of LEOs that militias wanted to create situations where they could get one agent, and then ambush others on their way to assist. Several entrapment scenarios had played on that fantasy to generate arrests. "You think so, Jack? Kinda ballsy, to take on a joint task force. Those guys couldn't organize an orgy at a French whorehouse."

"The militia of immediate interest to me seems to be doing quite well so far. And whoever is shooting at us is more than two dozen tea baggers with delusions of grandeur. Want me to make the call? We are practically out of ammunition and we need to negotiate while we can. I really don't want to use my last pistol round on myself" Gallagher was trying to get Gregory to understand they only had bad options left to them at this point.

"Go ahead" and the SAC seethed. The operation was a failure and he was on the hook for this. He had to think of a way out, and it would be easier to think without being shot at.

Gallagher held up a white writing tablet, the SAC got on the radio and told agents to cease fire. The HRT was visibly annoyed at the SAC. The SAC then handed the mike to Gallagher. The ASAC turned off transmission encryption.

"Attention militia, this is Special Agent Jack Gallagher. We request a cease fire for the purpose of negotiation, over"

About 30 seconds later came the answer "Request granted. Cease fire in effect. Parley in five minutes."

The SAC then asked Jack "Now what?"

"Let's get our people together, see who is hurt, and find out who we are dealing with." Gallagher suggested.

The agents were slow to move, none of them really trusted that the tea bagger militia would actually cease fire. The HRT guys were able to determine that their weapons had essentially been destroyed. Well, they would get another chance and then the tea bagger militia would pay.

"X-ray 47 this is X-ray 21 over." Roberts wondered what the commo chief had to say.

"X-ray 21 this is X-ray 47, over" Roberts answered the call.

"They request a ceasefire and parley, over" the commo chief informed Roberts.

Well, we may get out of this with a clean win yet. "Tell them request granted, cease fire in effect, parley in zero five mikes. Net call confirm cease fire." Each of the platoons, snipers, and others confirmed the cease fire. Roberts turned to his RTO. "You will accompany me, I'll brief the XO on the way. If there is an ex military guy there, he will note the PRC-119 and our equipment. Be mindful of that."

The request by the Fox news crew to come along was denied, but they were told that they could film at a distance. The brief to the XO was simple. "Any deception on their part – kill them all." Roberts and his RTO headed to the 2nd platoon leader and told him that they would head to the parlay from his position, and keep the Fox crew with him.

Five minutes passed and nothing happened. The SAC was irritated. "Where is this guy, Jack?"

"Assuming he is ex military, he is waiting for us. The military tradition is that the party requesting negotiations, sends the negotiating party halfway to the opposing party and stops. Then other party then comes forward." Gallagher answered.

"We're representatives of the US Government! Just who the hell does this guy think he is?" Gregory let his frustration show.

"Quite possibly someone at war with us and is currently winning." Gallagher was getting irritated, and wished he could have found a better way to remind the SAC how precarious their position was.

"Let's go." decided Gregory.

Both agents moved past the lead vehicle of the convoy and started west down the road. The SAC stopped after about 100 meters "That's enough."

Roberts and the RTO started forward after the agents stopped, It took about 20 seconds for them to come into view of the agents.

The agents were wearing the black vests and helmets common to US LE these days, but not much else in the tacticool department.

The agents now got a chance to size up their opposite number. They saw two soldiers approaching, and there was no doubt about that in Jack Gallagher's mind. They were dressed in woodland BDU, with what were probably current tan boots. Next on was the Individual Body Armor, also military woodland pattern, down to the MOLLE vest, pouches, the first aid kit was current issue, topping off the ensemble were the Kevlar helmets with night vision mount. Gallagher noted that the one who was obviously the commander was wearing aviator nomex gloves, long popular with armor crews. Both carried carbines, slung to the rear. Between the dress and tactics used against them, Gallagher was absolutely certain the soldier wearing those Captains bars and done this before, and for real.

Jack Gallagher was then struck with the thought that the captain was also doing it for real this time, too. Jack said what he thought – "You seem to have gotten the drop on us."

The SAC then had an epiphany. The tea bagger militia had been tipped off! They knew the task force was on the way, and they were waiting for him. And Jack seemed friendly enough to them – HE IS THE MOLE! The SAC then just knew the Jack Gallagher was probably one of those Oathkeepers! He had a traitor in is very task force. That explained everything, and that was how the SAC was going to get out of this. Jack Gallagher is going down. This calmed the SAC some.

Roberts responded, "So it seems. Special Agent Gallagher I presume?"

The SAC was now even more irritated. "I'm the Special Agent in Charge. Who are you?" Gregory snapped at Roberts.

Gallagher winced, the SAC really knows how to win friends and influence people he thought. Roberts saw Gallagher's expression and that told him much about the relationship between the two, and that Gallagher was probably the rational one.

"I'm the commander of the Borden County Militia." remarked Roberts. Gallagher sensed that was really true. Everybody recognized it, and it was unnecessary to inflate rank, bluff, or convince anyone of the fact. Then there was an awkward silence.

Then the SAC spoke, "OK let's get to it. It looks to me like we are pretty much at an impasse here. You have been successful in stopping us, and fortunately it looks like no one has been killed. Whatever is the issue between us will not be solved here today. We are going to call it a day and withdraw. Unfortunately we don't have any working vehicles, so it will be a few hours until we can be evacuated. Its OK with us if you stay in your current positions and watch us leave." The SAC knew that the DoJ had taken almost everybody they had in a five state region for this operation, and whatever help was on the way, would not be enough. They would have to try again, later and with much more force. And next time, the Government would have the element of surprise. If the militia guys hung around, there would have a better idea as to how many of them there were and how well the tea baggers were equipped.

Neither agent was prepared for the response: "That option is not available to you." Roberts stated.

Roberts had the upper hand and was now in control. Fox news had witnessed the action, and the fact that the feds had asked for a cease fire in order to negotiate. No matter what happened next, it was clear who had won. The only question now was how big the win was going to be.

Finally, Gallagher asked, "What do you mean by that?"

"There are two options available to you. Option one is unconditional surrender. Option two is to use whatever means you have remaining at hand to fight and die, right here, right now. You will have 30 seconds to decide. If you fail to make a decision at the end of the time given, I will assume option two and act accordingly." Roberts then made a display of holding up his watch. "Time begins now."

The SAC was crushed. Gallagher tried to salvage something from the situation. "How do we know you won't just shoot us?"

To make the decision easier, Roberts told him, "First, if we were going to shoot you, we would not have wasted the time and ammunition we have so far. We simply would have shot you. Second, I have a Fox news crew with me and summary executions of government agents play badly, even on that network. Third, you have my positive assurance that we will treat you better than you would have treated us in the same circumstances. But that last one really isn't saying much is it? Time has expired."

While every fiber in his career oriented being said otherwise, the SAC almost involuntarily said "We surrender."

Gallagher immediately realized what a disaster this was. It was one thing to bag eight IRS agents who thought they were going to shut down a rogue bank. Those guys had no idea what they were walking into. But this operation was different. The militia who pulled that operation, who were going to be arrested by the DoJ, had in effect arrested the DoJ. And a national news network had footage of the whole thing. While ABC might sit on it, you could bet money that this was going to get out eventually and it was going to be bad: 'Texas Arrests Federal Government' would be the headline on every tea bagger website. And at some point, even Fox news would pick up on it big time just like Fast and Furious.

There was no doubt Washington was going to go ballistic over this. Not only were the Texans making the federal government look like fools, it would not be long before real criminals got the idea that they could get away with defiance as well. A minor crisis that rational adults should have been able to solve was now going to have shattering implications for the United States. Jack Gallagher could not retire soon enough. But first, Gallagher would have to get out of this situation.

Roberts reached down and unholstered the 1911A1 pistol he was carrying, drew it and took the safety off. "Gentlemen, we will begin by you handing over your weapons."

Chapter 14

Internment Operations

A Department of Justice Joint Task Force had just surrendered to a local Texas militia, unknown to anyone outside of Borden County.

Gregory and Gallagher had not brought long arms to the negotiation, only their service pistols. Both reached down to hand over their weapons.

"Slowly please, gentlemen. You know the routine." Roberts' RTO had moved his carbine around to the front, and there was the click of the safety being disengaged.

The agents made a show of moving slowly, and using only the thumb and forefinger to bring their pistols out of their holsters, and hold the weapons with barrel pointed toward the ground for Roberts to take. The pistols were than handed to the RTO.

"Do I need to search you?" Roberts asked.

Gallagher replied, "That won't be necessary."

Roberts decided search Gregory anyway. It was an established communist procedure to humiliate a superior in front of a subordinate. Not a bad tool for working on prisoners to help break the chain of command.

That had been noticed by Gallagher who then asked "You prior service, captain?"

"A long, long time ago, in a galaxy far, far away." Roberts told him.

That answer made Gallagher even more curious. He said "I was in Schweinfurt. Those were good times, you knew who the enemy was."

All he got out of Roberts was "I was to the southeast of 3 ID." He knew former military guys would recognize each other, but he wasn't interested in giving out too much information.

That confirmed it for Gallagher. The militia commander had been in either the Second Armored Cavalry Regiment or 1st Armored Division. He would have bet that the guy did border patrol watching the Warsaw Pact forces back in the days of the Cold War. Units going eye to eye with the Soviets were not where the Army assigned its idiots. The investigator in Gallagher pushed for more information. "So, how did you end up in a militia?"

Roberts stated "I was aided and abetted by agencies of the United States Government. Let your profilers chew on that. Interview over."

Gallagher then realized that he had been told what is was that the captain wanted him to know.

By then, they had walked back into view of most of the agents who had gathered back near their vehicles. Two agents were injured as a result of the wreck of the lead SUV, and two had bullet wounds, not life threatening, although the HRT agent's wounds were not inconsequential.

"Stop here" Roberts told them. "Get on your radio to your people and tell them the following: Leave all weapons, ammunition, and equipment by the vehicles. Then move north of the road running east and west a distance of 25 meters. Get on their knees, ankles crossed, and hands on the head. We will then process them as prisoners."

Roberts held his left hand out for the RTO to hand him the mike. "All X-ray elements, this is X-ray 47. We will be processing prisoners. They will leave all weapons and equipment by the vehicles, proceed 25 meters toward the Romeo element, and get on their knees. The Romeo element will cover the prisoners. When the prisoners are in position, the Echo element will move forward to the vehicles. When the Echo element reaches the vehicles, the Oscar element will assume covering the prisoners, and the Romeo element will move to the northernmost vehicle and start equipment collection. Further orders will follow."

Roberts then told Gregory, "Make the call and get them moving." Roberts motioned the second platoon forward, so they would be better able to cover the prisoners. The XO, and First Sergeant came forward with second platoon. They and the second platoon leader came up to Roberts.

Roberts addressed the second platoon leader "Get your men behind them as they clear the vehicles, so I can move first platoon out of the way of a crossfire. They have some injured that third platoon will have to handle, keep an eye out until third platoon has the vehicles cleared. Top, these two are the leader and second in command, take them with you and get a prisoner count.

We are going to march them to the county jail, although before we get there I expect transportation to take us to the detention facility. XO – I need you, supply section, and commo section to pick up the phones and wire, bring our vehicles down here, and start collecting all weapons, ammo and equipment. Tell the reporters that after they get their footage to see me, and we will discuss the subject of how they get their news back to the world."

The agents were not in too much of a hurry to leave their weapons behind, and made no hurry to do so. The platoon leader of first platoon was not satisfied with the amount of energy being expended to comply with the surrender requirements. He selected an agent that was dawdling too long by a pile of weapons, and fired one round that impacted almost two feet away from the agent. The energizer bunny then took hold and that spurred movement away from the vehicles, then the agents started to form the line on their knees.

Roberts had his cell phone out and made the first call to the sheriff. "Roberts here, Sheriff Connors. It's over and we are processing prisoners. Want to come by, place them under arrest, and figure out where we take them?"

"I'm on the way. Anybody killed? How many did you bag?" Connors wanted to know.

"None killed, some injured agents, a serious gunshot wounded agent, so a couple of ambulances will do. Don't have a final count yet, but a couple hundred." Roberts reported.

"You can't keep this up. The county is going to have more prisoners than residents at the rate you're going." Connors joked.

"I need to clean up the site before their friends come to visit." Roberts said to the Sheriff.

"I understand, they are going to the school – that is going to be the detention facility. I have a couple of school busses that will be following me." Connors had been setting up the detention facility.

"Thanks, see you in a few." Roberts was now back to business.

Next call was to McMasters "Roberts here, we have a victory. Get ready for every media outlet in the world to head for Borden County. Now for the bad news – we need to guard, house, feed, and care for some 200 prisoners, and the guard force. But I can discuss that with you this afternoon." It was important to let McMasters know, not just because he was a director of Free Texas, but as one of the county commissioners, this was now his problem to deal with as well.

"Thank God, any of our guys hurt? How many feds?" McMasters wanted to know.

"All of ours are OK, looks like a few feds injured with no life threatening injuries." Roberts reported to Ed.

"Now all Hell breaks loose, but in a good way, right?" Ed asked.

"Right" confirmed Roberts.

"You know you have my full support. You have more than earned it. I know you must be busy, where do you think you'll be this afternoon?" McMasters asked.

"County seat, we will probably hold them at the football field, but I have a favor to ask." Roberts answered.

"Anything" McMasters promised.

"We are doing our best to move all of the people and equipment out of here as fast as we can. Some time later today, I expect somebody from the feds to look for a missing assault force, and I want them to find these abandoned vehicles. After a minute or two of them looking around, I want somebody with a non military caliber weapon to shoot out the visitors back window, and scare them back to where they came from." Roberts requested.

"You got it, anything else?" Ed was starting to select a candidate for the task.

"We'll talk this afternoon" Roberts suggested.

"OK bye" and Ed hung up the phone.

The platoon leader of third platoon approached Roberts with two people in tow. "These two claim to be reporters with ABC news. Here are their cell phones. Found a camera, too."

"We are media and here are our credentials" snapped the taller of the two in best New Yawker speech.

Roberts thought that implied and unstated at the end of that sentence was - you cretinous mouth breathing knuckle dragging tea bagging militia moron. Just for fun he replied "I could order that off the internet."

"You will return our property and let us go immediately. You constitution guys only believe in guns, not the first amendment." demanded Brett Williams of ABC News.

Roberts motioned for the XO to come over. "Here is what is going to happen. You will be detained until such time as I can determine your status as actual media and entitled to protections afforded to the press. If your story checks out, your property will be returned to you, then you will be released, and you may report whatever you wish. And just for your information, you are trespassing on private property, people have been shot for that in this state or for much less. There are no taxis here, and it is a very long walk to any form of public transportation, not even an Uber driver with a Prius is to be had for over 50 miles. And you have been scooped by the Fox news crew accredited to this unit. You will now accompany this officer."

The sheriff arrived in his truck, followed by two school busses and two ambulances. The company supply section had the pickups down by the column of vehicles, first platoon was loading the vehicles, four agents were laid out. The two from the first vehicle with some broken ribs and minor concussions, one with a grazing gun shot wound to the lower leg, who was now known as hop along, and the agent shot in the hands now referred to as mittens. The medics in first and third platoon had found the feds first aid kits and used them on the injured agents. Mittens was about to get an IV when the ambulances pulled in.

Sheriff Connors walked directly to Roberts. "What do you need the county sheriff to do in his official capacity?"

Roberts stated "The four injured ones over there – do what you would normally do for arrestees who need medical treatment. I know that will take them out of the county, and at some point a federal judge will very probably order them released and the local authorities will likely do it. That is OK, I can afford to lose them and use it for political gain. Then we need for you arrest the other 236 and transport them to the stadium or jail for processing and then the stadium. I'm sure the news would love to cover the perp walk from the jail to the stadium. I suspect a couple of their FBI buddies will come to visit shortly, and I want nothing but wrecks to be here when they arrive. Then your favorite towing company will have some business and send the bill to the owners of these public nuisances."

"Anything else?" asked Sheriff Connors.

"One thing and it is going to be a wild one." Roberts ventured.

"Do tell." the Sheriff wanted to know.

Roberts then told of his plan. "After you arrest them, I am going to detain them in my role a commander of a militia, and charge them with war crimes under the Geneva Conventions. This will require a military tribunal, to determine the status of the detained personnel and so forth. It may take some of the pressure off you."

"You can do that?" Sheriff Connors was surprised by the plan.

"It is a little fuzzy, but let's see how the fed gov likes a system that might not be subject to the rules of federal criminal procedure. I won't do anything illegal." Roberts reassured him.

"War crimes like what?" Connors wanted to know.

"Well, by now most of the county probably thinks World War III is underway, but seriously, in our military capacity, we are combatants under the terms of the Geneva Conventions. You, and all other police agencies are considered non combatants. It is a war crime for non combatants to engage combatants. A bit of a stretch, but we will see what some legal minds think and have some fun in the process. After that they get turned over to you and the Texas legal system." Roberts said.

"I'll support you." affirmed Sheriff Connors.

Sheriff Connors then arrested the four injured agents for official oppression, assault with a deadly weapon, disorderly conduct, and criminal trespass. The agents were then loaded into the ambulances. At that point the two ambulances departed for the nearest hospital.

The platoons were not quite done with searching and placing zip ties on the prisoners. The command group's RTOs had the ABC reporters on ice. This gave Roberts a few minutes with the command group. He asked for Sheriff Connors to attend. The commo chief reported that the field phones and wire had been secured, the cell phone blocker and radio frequency jamming discontinued, and he could put up a short range drone for observation, if needed. There was still no evidence of enemy drone activity. The first Sergeant reported 236 prisoners taken, no injuries or other loss to the company. He reminded Roberts there were no provisions made for lunch. The XO reported that the vehicle search was done, and everything was loaded in the pickups. The supply sergeant asked what did Roberts want done with the captured material.

Roberts laid out the course of action. "Here is the plan for the next six hours. The XO takes the supply section, commo section, and first platoon – they need a break – as the quartering party to the county jail and school athletic complex. The prisoners will be processed at the jail, but as the cells are full of IRS guys, we will house the prisoners on the football field, the track surface will be the deadline. Set up first as the initial guard force for that, we will let Fox get shots of the perp walk from the jail to the field, filming the prisoners from the rear, so their faces can not be made out – Geneva Convention rules about subjecting prisoners to curiosity and ridicule apply.

We will house the company under the stands between the field and the gym. Supply see about setting up operations in the locker room, the other locker room as company CP. Inventory the captured material – it is now ours as spoils of war. I'll tell you about disposition of it later tonight. Commo – set up a SB-22 at the CP and run phones to the HQ sections, the cantonment area, and probably stadium press box as the main guard post. Maybe a SB-933 in the pressbox and other phones to each guard post. To the extent possible, use spares on the guard posts, so the platoons can retain as much of their equipment as possible.

Top, it looks like four serials in the busses to get all of the prisoners, and the other platoons moved. Take them to the jail and off load ricky tick, to get everybody out of here. You and I will be last ones out. When I arrive at the jail, I'll release the Fox crew, and hold ABC for a while to make sure Fox has the story out there first. About 30 minutes to an hour after our arrival, and after our good sheriff verifies the pajama boys there are really reporters, they can figure out how they are going to get back to New York.

I'll try to work a plan with the county emergency board on feeding. We have just more than doubled the population of Gail, they don't even feed this many kids in the school cafeteria every day. Maybe the school cafeteria kitchen can handle the load, maybe not. We will certainly need our support folks from now on. Guidons at 1800 at the CP to discuss longer term operations. Now, I think the sheriff and myself need to address the prisoners if there are no questions, and Sheriff Connors agrees.

We keep the weapons, ammunition, and radios as spoils of war. Sheriff Connors gets the rest of the captured material."

The duty agent in Dallas had been unable to contact the JTF, or find anyone who could contact them. He called the Lubbock field office and got the ASAC's secretary. He asked if there has been any news from the JTF and she replied no one had called in. The duty agent was worried, there should have been confirmation by now that the suspects had been taken into custody. He asked if there were some agents that could go out to perform a check on the JTF. There were only two agents left in the office today because they were scheduled to testify in court this morning, therefore they could not go on the raid. He requested that they be sent out ASAP, and to then report back to him.

The duty agent dreaded making the call to Washington, but at this stage knew he had to. To his surprise, he was put through to the Director. "Sir, we have lost contact with the JTF. I had one conversation earlier with SAC Gregory who reported they had been ambushed and were under attack. He requested assistance, but almost every agent available went with the JTF. There were two agents left at the Lubbock office who were in court this morning, and are being sent out to investigate. I checked with ATF, and they can not reach their agents either. That is all I have as of now, sir."

"Thank you and call back immediately as soon as more information is developed." The Director then turned to his brain trust, who had heard the report over speakerphone. "What do you make of this?"

"Well, he used the words ambush and attack in the report, so we should conclude our agents were fired on by that militia down there in Texas. So we have to be prepared to deal with dead or seriously injured agents and criminals. It will help with our initiative on gun violence, and may be the push we need for at least an assault weapon ban if not a ban on firearms in general. At least the President will be happy about that part of the operation." One of the Director's aides posited.

"I agree. We need to get out in front of this, maybe not you or the AG yet as we don't have enough detail. But a presser to get the message out there should happen. I think there was a reporter along on this, and he will have the visuals. So if we go with the presser at 3, we can get the story out there, and fill in the detail for the evening news. That should help build support for taking down the militia movement and those allied organizations. The IRS is sure to help, as we are recovering eight of their agents." contributed another aide.

"I'd be careful about mentioning recovery of the IRS agents as we don't yet know that we have them back. Also when we mention that we have had agents shot at, the families are going to get worried, and we might get some negative coverage about leaving them in the dark on this." Replied the first aide.

"Right, so we go with announcing the JTF went to recover the IRS agents, has been fired on by right wing militia extremists, illustrating the danger to law enforcement caused by heavily armed militias. Therefore, as a result of this action we expect to take further action to protect Americans from gun violence and this shows the impact of the failure of Congress to address this issue. We will have more information later in the day, as the JTF checks in. Have media relations go with that, we may know more by presser time." decided the Director.

Meanwhile the ABC news producer who sent Brett Williams to Texas with the FBI was curious to know what happened to his reporter. He called up his contact over at Department of Justice. "What have you guys done with my reporter? He called in that they were fired on. Are you guys sitting on him?" He was told that, yes, the team had been fired on and that there would be a press conference at 3, and the word was being put out to the media. "My guy better have his footage and you bastards better not have given this to NBC, or I'll have your ass." He then rang the copy editor – we have breaking news to give to the talking head on now. He then had his assistant make calls to the Brady center to Prevent Gun Violence and the Southern Poverty Law Center to get then lined up for special segments on the evening news about the danger posed by militias with automatic weapons, and to hopefully get them booked on the news before the other networks did.

At 1:50 PM Eastern Time, ABC network news went with a breaking story. A Joint Task Force led by the FBI with the mission of recovering kidnapped IRS agents has been fired on by a right wing extremist Texas militia. Sources reported the agents were under heavy gunfire from automatic weapons, and more information was expected soon from an ABC reporter who was on the scene with the FBI.

Roberts was just about to get on the last bus rotation with the remaining prisoners and guards when his phone rang. It was McMasters "You seen the news?"

"I'm a bit busy right now." Roberts responded.

"Just heard that ABC reported on the shootout this morning." Ed told Roberts.

"I have their reporters here incommunicado. What did they say?" Roberts wanted to know what ABC was broadcasting.

"Mostly an anti gun right wing tea bagger rant with the mention that the FBI is having a press conference about the action at 2 Central." Ed summarized.

Roberts was thinking through the implications. "It will be interesting to find out what the FBI knows that we don't. Great heads up on that. I'll have the reporters out of here by then. If they file their reports while the press conference is still ongoing, that could create an awkward situation for some people in Washington. And can you visit us at the school gym about 6ish? Tell people to start watching the news in about 30 minutes"

"Sure." Ed confirmed.

Roberts made sure that the site was left clean.

The only two remaining field agents from the Lubbock field office had just made it to the Borden County border. After getting out of court, they decided not to dirty up one of their own cars with the bugs on the windshield and the dirt of west Texas driving, but went to the GSA motor pool to check out a G-ride. All the SUVs were already out, but they got a sedan, which normally would be reserved for somebody two grades above them. Life was good. They missed having to get up too early in the morning to go deal with that Borden County mess, except to find out why nobody seemed to be able to find a functioning radio or a cell phone tower that wasn't dead.

Freedonia was too new of a settlement to make it onto a map yet, but the agents knew where to go, as they had listened to yesterday's brief at the office. Still nobody answered the damn radio. As they approached the intersection of Highway 180 and the farm to Market road to Freedonia, the reason for their failure to communicate with the Joint Task Force became clear.

"HOLY SHIT!" Except for the fact that none of the vehicles had burned, the Borden County Militia had created a scene that resembled the "Highway of Death" out of Kuwait City in the first Gulf War. All of the people and movable equipment of the Joint task Force had vanished. The G-ride stopped a bit short of the last vehicle, while attention naturally focused on the bus, which was nose into a hole, and rear axle in the air. The agents got out, and as they approached the nearest vehicle, there was the sound of the rear glass and left rear window exploding from the impact of one round of .300 Win mag.

"We're outta here." And the agents scrambled into the G-ride, turned a bit too wide, picking up some debris in the right front fender and hit the gas for Lubbock. Had the maneuver been observed by a Trooper of the Texas Department of Public Safety, his report would have noted a display of acceleration at a high rate of speed.

The radio in the G-ride still worked. "They have been wiped out. There is nothing left, and we barely got out of there alive! They shot out the back of the vehicle" The agents did not have time to notice that the only blood left behind was on the HRT team van by mittens. Only when asked how many bodies they saw did the agents realize that the site was picked clean.

This fact was the subject of much discussion between Lubbock, Dallas, and Washington. That the militia would want to carry off their own dead and wounded was understandable. That would provide important information about them, although the FBI was now reasonably sure who was involved – it must be practically the whole county. And that was going to be a problem. That they carried off the agents' weapons and equipment was understandable too, that militia now had improved their armament as the FBI knew militias hardly possessed anything more than ARs at best.

But why carry off the agents' bodies. What point did that serve? Nobody seemed to be able to offer a good reason – photograph for propaganda – they could have done that at the scene and make it more spectacular. Not give away the type of weapons they had used to kill the agents? The speculation continued as press conference time grew near. It was bad enough that the FBI had lost 240 agents along with other federal agencies, but not being able to say what happened to them at a press conference was going to be even worse.

One of the Director's brain trust summed up the situation thus, "We're screwed. We need to get everybody we can get down there."

The militia was now establishing operations in the county seat to be near the jail, courthouse, and school complex. Roberts went over to the Fox reporters. "I apologize for holding you so long, but I had to get operations close enough to set here before I could let you report what happened. Here are your cell phones and you are free to go. Before you go, I want to give you an update. ABC has gone with the story of a shootout down here. It is clear from their reporting, that they did not get any real detail about what had happened from their crew on scene, whom we still hold.

The FBI is holding a press conference at 2 PM, which I'm sure your station will confirm as soon as you call them. The footage you have will be the first knowledge anyone has that we have captured the raid party. This will give you tremendous advantage in coverage for the rest of the day. I can only hope that the reward had been worth the inconvenience to you. I'm sure there will be requests for interviews and such later, and your cooperation will put you at the front of the line. Good luck to you and have a safe journey."

The Fox crew beat feet to their van. If they drove back to Lubbock, the press conference would still be underway or over by the time they reached the station. Roberts guessed they would stop along the way and connect back to the station ASAP to break the news. He hoped they would call in the report and show the footage after the FBI presser, but one in his position could only hope to influence events. Control of the press was not possible.

The Fox news crew was on the phone to the station before the van's engine started. The station manager confirmed that the information Roberts had provided was correct. Then the reporter dropped the bomb. They were there for the whole thing and had it on video. There were 36 minutes of battle, a few minutes of the two leaders talking, ended by two FBI guys handing pistols to the militia commander. Then there was the scene of 240 agents of the US Government being arrested by the county sheriff and being processed as prisoners. In all, well over an hour of visuals. The station manager made the reporter confirm no deaths and all agents captured. ABC reports were giving a different impression. The report was dictated, reconfirmed, and the station manager said it would go to national ASAP. There would be plenty of time to edit the footage for the evening news.

There had been a couple of the school's TVs brought into the gym as word was getting around the county of the adventures of the Borden County Militia. A good number of Texans were of the mindset that all they want is to be left alone and lead their lives as they saw fit. It was becoming clearer every day, that any employee of the federal government would be prudent to avoid setting foot in Borden County, Texas. The FBI presser was on and one TV set was tuned to Fox News Channel, the national TV network of Texas, and the other to ABC for amusement, scorn, and derision. Most of the company that was not on duty guarding the detainees (they were the sheriff's prisoners, but the militia's detainees) were having a look.

Both ABC and Fox cut live to the Department of Justice press conference. It started a few minutes late. The DoJ PR flack read a prepared statement, stating that a Joint Task Force of the DoJ had deployed to Texas to rescue the eight IRS agents being held by a rogue sheriff and a right wing extremist militia. The heroic agents were taken under fire by the militia using their heavy assault weapons. The militia had caught the agents while still in a vehicle convoy, and the raid had failed. The PR flack then went into the standard gun control rant on assault weapons; Congressional failure to enact common sense gun control measures, how the President had tried to avert such a tragedy and so on. The question was now whether the press was going to eat that brand of dog food.

Roberts told the XO to bring the pajama boys from ABC in, they would want to see this. As the reporters entered, the prepared statement had ended and it was question time. The first two questioners bought the party line, and the questions had to do with another proposed assault weapons ban and if it should only be limited to semi automatics. Fox flashed a Breaking News graphic on the screen. Roberts pointed to the ABC screen and said "Kill that, we need to hear Fox."

The announcer stated "This just in from Fox local affiliate KJTV 34 in Lubbock. A Department of Justice Joint Task Force sent to obtain release of eight IRS agents and to arrest a local militia unit has instead been arrested by the sheriff of Borden County and are in the custody of the Borden County Militia. This occurred after a 35 minute gun battle witnessed by Fox34 news. The total number of federal agents captured is 240 and there were 4 injured government agents with no deaths on either side. Injuries were reported to be non life threatening. Video taken at the scene will be shown within the hour as soon as the news crew returns to the station."

Most of the militiamen cheered. They had won a victory, and the whole world was going to know it. Roberts motioned to the two ABC reporters. "Here are your phones, and you can pick up your camera on the way out." He mused that as they say in the UK, the cat has been set amongst the pigeons. Their camera had been placed by the door of the gym. As soon as they were out the door, Brett Williams was on the phone to New York.

Back at the press conference, there was finally a question about the agents on the raid and how many casualties. The non answer to the question was that they did not yet have a full accounting of everyone on the scene, and in any case policy would be to notify families before the public announcement of any loss.

For the last hour, family and friends of agents had been calling, even agents that were not on the raid were getting calls wanting to know if they were all right and knew anything about the raid. For the family and friends of 240 agents, there had been no answer, and calls were coming into the offices. That information had not made it to the media yet.

The Fox News national reporter on the DC circuit was at the presser, and at best Fox might get one question in toward the end. That was just the way it was. An incoming text message caught his attention – it had the substance of the news reported by the Lubbock station that had gone national. He knew he now had the question that was going to be on every sound bite for the next three hours, but he had to get called on. A FBI suit walked up to the PR flack and whispered something into her ear. She then announced that she had to meet with the Director urgently, and unfortunately could take no more questions.

The three majors and CNN were eating the government dog food. They played up the right wing extremist gun control angle with crocodile tears over the fate of the agents who were now called missing, as if they had disappeared into the Bermuda Triangle. The usual suspects were brought out to inflame public opinion for more gun control and regulation of internet radio and other "tea bagger' communications.

Fox repeated its' Breaking News announcement and then started to promote the film to be shown at the top of the hour. As expected, ABC was the first crack in the narrative being parroted by the authorized journalists. ABC now reported that some agents had been captured by the militia and the fate of the agents was unknown. And another outpouring of crocodile tears ensued.

Top of the hour was also shift change for the guard force, so now first platoon could get a cold one and watch some tube. Fox News delivered. The local news crew that had been on the scene for the battle, proceeded to set the stage. They had been invited to a militia training exercise with permission to film. Roberts had been prepared for the reporters to let the cat out of the bag that the militia had been tipped off – that would just plant fear, uncertainty, and doubt in the minds of the DoJ that someone was leaking info to the tea baggers which would be perfectly OK. In fact some anxiety on the part of the federal government about their operational security might make them more hesitant to try another raid.

But, he noted the reporters had protected a source. That would give them the opportunity to get more news first. Then FOX cut to the film of the vehicles making the turn onto the road to Freedonia, with the two loud pops of the road surface dropping. The next scene was perfect, a back view of Roberts, handset in hand, demanding the surrender of the agents. Then there was gunfire, and visuals of vehicles being hit and agents scrambling away from the vehicles. Roberts noted it was impossible to tell who fired first. After some 45 seconds of that (TV audiences are quickly bored), the scene focused on the firefight around the van, mittens getting hit and falling down.

That won't make us many friends there, thought Roberts. Then the next scene was Gallagher waving the white tablet, and firing coming to a stop. Now the parley between two agents and two militiamen was on the screen, and the two agents were being shown handing their pistols to one of the militiamen. The next cut was to a scene of agents leaving the vehicles and lining up on their knees. They next showed the search and tying of the agents. Next scene was of mittens and hop along being loaded into an ambulance. Then the screen showed Sheriff Connors placing the agents under arrest, and then the last scene was of the perp walk from the jail toward the stadium. Then Fox cut back to the reporters and started the self congrats of really being dedicated to covering the story. It would be another cable ratings bonanza for Fox. Anybody seeing that footage got one unmistakable message – the United States Government had just had its ass handed to it.

"All right, you guys know how the movie ends, let's get back to work." Roberts announced. Morale was high, not for just the usual reason for having gone into harm's way and survived, but having not lost a man, won a victory, and now the world knew about it. They had confidence in themselves as a unit. But, this was not yet over. It had barely begun.

Roberts decided the next thing he needed to do was to call the morning host of Rampaging Elephants, the internet radio outlet that had been very friendly to Free Texas and the militias in general. They had heard about the raid and would like to have him on soonest. He promised them first interview at 6:30 that evening. He wanted to get the media message sorted out. Rampaging Elephants and the local Fox station had the connections with what was happening in Borden County. They would figure out how to make use of it.

McMasters called. "I just saw the whole thing on Fox. You guys did great. Where do we go from here?" Roberts told him that he was having a leaders meeting a 6, and if he, the Free Texas board, and as many of the county guys as he could get could come by before, it would be helpful. "How about 5?"

"Great, now I have some troops to feed." Roberts noted.

"Way ahead of you, it is on the way." McMasters announced.

"Thanks" and now Roberts might get a break for an hour.

The sad pandas in Washington, DC were in full panic mode. Directors called the AG. The White House called the AG. The brain trust headed for the situation room, The President was not there. He had underlings to deal with this disaster. Discussion turned from call in every FBI agent in the country, to use of the military, to wait 24 hours to see if the story got traction anywhere other than Fox. They did agree on one action item. Federal Court orders to get the four injured agents out of Texas. That would show the President and the public that they were managing the issue. And they suggested the President call the Governor of Texas. They needed to find out on which side the Governor of Texas was on before doing anything themselves that they might be able to get the Governor to do for them.

By 5 PM, McMasters, Greenlow, the other directors of Free Texas, and the county commissioners court was at the gym, in the what was now the Command Post of the Borden County Militia. Roberts laid out the situation. "Gentlemen thank you for being here. Here is the situation, what needs to be done from my perspective, and what I intend to do. First, we are using the school facilities, which is disruptive to education. A longer term solution may be needed which will probably need some 100 acres for prisoner holding, and essentially a militia camp for as many as 800 troops. The immediate need is for shelter for 240 detainees, and porta johns – we now have to rotate them in and out of the gym using the guard force. Same goes for the company. We are going to need tents and tarps. Next is feeding operations, whatever the capacity is of the cafeteria here at the school, we will probably exceed it. I ask the county to take that on, as it will be county resources that manage it, and you may have a link to the state Adjutant General, to see what the state may have in terms of military equipment we might use – declare a county emergency and notify the Governor.

Next is the media circus which you can expect to start to arrive shortly. The good news is that there are no overnight facilities in the county, so they will probably stay in Lubbock and we only see them from early morning to 10 PM newscast. Somebody who wants to make some money might open up a café and whatever else will give them someplace to be during the day. How lucky we are that there is no building code compliance or health inspector to hold that up from happening tomorrow.

Also like at Bundy Ranch, we are going to get volunteers of every stripe, which will create its own problems, mainly for me, but likely more strain on the facilities. Probably somebody from the county commissioners and definitely from Free Texas needs to be the media minder. They will want stories, background, people to talk to, and the story will be anything from local bubbas who don't like the Federal Government to Texas is in revolution and is going to leave the United States."

McMasters broke in "That is already out there"

Roberts continued "Yes but the questions will be what is your purpose and objective, so you need to give an answer that makes some sense to even a reporter."

Then one of the commissioners from a family that had been in the county for generations broke in, "Good question. What are you doing?"

Roberts went into lecture mode "My strategic objective is to give the people of Texas the opportunity to decide what type of relationship Texas should have with the US Government. Is Texas a mere subsidiary of the US government, is Texas a sovereign state in a federation of sovereign states, or has the US government acted in such a way that Texas can no longer maintain any satisfactory relationship with the federal government? I think the question is of the gravest import for our future as a people and needs to be discussed.

This brings me to the tactical objective. I will convene a military tribunal to determine the status of the detainees under the Geneva Conventions – more specifically to decide whether the US government has invaded Texas and engaged in war with the Texas Military Forces. Yes I'm stretching it somewhat, but in effect we will put the US government on trial for violating the US Constitution. Something the legal system should have taken care of a long time ago, but has totally failed to do. And the media of the world will be here to cover it"

McMasters was the first to speak, "Nobody can say that you don't think big."

Roberts said "And all of the logistics of this is going to be expensive. We need a mechanism to solicit donations, and at some point we all have to get back to our day jobs."

"I wonder what Austin is going to do?" Ted Greenlow asked on no one in particular.

"So do I." answered Roberts. "We are now the mouse that roared."

Chapter 15

Constitution Class

Later that evening, Roberts had the internees gathered together so that he could address them. He expected they would find his announcement even more disturbing than their current predicament.

The United States is a signatory, with some reservations, to the Geneva Conventions of the conduct of warfare. As a treaty, its provisions take precedence over any federal or state law, subject only to the US Constitution. There were some interesting provisions contained therein.

Article 3 of the Geneva Convention extends the provisions of the Geneva Conventions to conflicts not of an international character, if both parties in the conflict agree to abide by the conventions, Before deploying, Roberts had sent an email to the International Committee of the Red Cross, from the Borden County Militia, the notification that the unit had acceded to the Geneva Conventions, subject to the same reservations as the United States of America. Under the terms of Article 49 of the First Geneva Convention, all parties to the Convention have the authority to "take measures necessary for the suppression of all acts contrary to the provisions of the present Convention other than the grave breaches defined in the following Article."

"In all circumstances, the accused persons shall benefit by safeguards of proper trial and defence, which shall not be less favourable than those provided by Article 105 and those following of the Geneva Convention relative to the Treatment of Prisoners of War of August 12, 1949."

This would form the basis of the tribunal to come. The raid party was not only under arrest by the sheriff of Borden County, they were about to be accused of a breach of the Geneva Conventions. Every member of the militia, except for the volunteers who had joined last night, carried a Geneva Conventions identity card, the US military uses this as the military ID, and Roberts still carried his, noting his POW category as Class III in case of capture. Every person entitled to be recognized as a combatant under the Conventions was supposed to carry such identification. Law enforcement officers do not carry such identification, because they have the status of non combatants under the conventions.

Article 4 of the Third Geneva Convention made the Borden County Militia combatants, and thus entitled them to the treatment as POWs via Section 2: "Members of other militias and members of other volunteer corps, including those of organized resistance movements, belonging to a Party to the conflict and operating in or outside their own territory, even if this territory is occupied, provided that such militias or volunteer corps, including such organized resistance movements, fulfil the following conditions:

a) that of being commanded by a person responsible for his subordinates;

b) that of having a fixed distinctive sign recognizable at a distance;

c) that of carrying arms openly;

d) that of conducting their operations in accordance with the laws and customs of war."

This was the reason the Borden County Militia was organized, uniformed, and trained as it was. Even if the State of Texas did not recognize them as part of the Texas Military Forces, the United States government in this case had to if it obeyed the Geneva Conventions. The agents were about to be informed that they were now being held by the Borden County Militia in accordance of Article 5 of the Third Geneva Convention, to wit: "Should any doubt arise as to whether persons having committed a belligerent act and having fallen into the hands of the enemy belong to any of the categories enumerated in Article 4, such persons shall enjoy the protection of the present Convention until such time as their status has been determined by a competent tribunal." Until such time as the tribunal made a determination of the status of the internees, they would receive treatment as prisoners of war.

The Fourth Geneva Convention applies to the treatment of civilian persons by combatants. If found not to be combatants, it would allow a tribunal to use the laws of the United States against the internees. In short, Roberts would then use the Military Commissions Act of 2009 against the US government. Of course the accused would claim that acting as agents of the US government, Article 3 exempted them from having the Conventions used against them. Court TV would have nothing on this show.

The agents had been gathered to one side of the field, and Roberts spoke to then from the first row in the stands. He informed them that they were now interned pending a determination of their status as either combatants and entitled to be treated as prisoners of war, or as belligerents who had no such protection and would be prosecuted as such. They were informed that their internment would be reported to the Red Cross in the morning. Appropriate shelter and facilities would be forthcoming as soon as could be effected. That should have some work on their morale he thought. While escape was a concern, there was almost nothing but dirt for 50 miles. The agents had nowhere to go.

Roberts had been going at it hard for 24 hours, and was starting to tire by the time of the 1800 leaders call. "Biggest thing right now is for Top, we should have tentage and porta johns on the way so the internees don't have to rotate into the gym for latrine breaks, which will help on security. They get the first tents, if we get some GPs or TEMPER tents, that would help, as we could then get cots and some life support in there later. We will have the school cafeteria going to shifts, so people will be eating at off times.

XO, I expect some volunteers will start showing up on the order of Bundy Ranch. You will need to collect up volunteers, and get some idea of who is prior service and can be used as NCOs with a view of forming volunteers into new platoons. When we get there, each of the platoon leaders will run two platoons, one of ours and one of volunteers to stretch the manpower. Assuming things start to stabilize in the morning, I'll release a platoon to go home, shower, and get some rest. Pass the word to see if there are families that will be willing to put up guests. Time to run the HQ as a two shift 24 hour operation, 12 on and 12 off.

If commo can monitor for radio or drone electronic communications, that is the main task, a secondary is to extend net connectivity around here if you can. I'm assuming every full time news organization in the world is on its way here. Supply - we have good news and bad news. As I'm a bad news first guy, you will have to take on the inbound supplies, We want tentage, cots, food, uniforms, field gear, weapons, and ammo for our force. How much is going to come in is a mystery, and it has to be stored and accounted for to the generous people we hope will support us. Good news is after you inventory the captured weapons and equipment. Every member of the unit present for duty today gets one handgun, one long arm, and associated magazines. The rest is now company property for issue as needed. Selection goes by order of rank.

Anything else? Get some sleep."

It was time for the Rampaging Elephants interview, and Roberts gave a run down of the operation that took place that day to the audience, Rampaging Elephants was breaking into scheduled programming for the interview. He ended with an appeal for funds, equipment and volunteers, especially cooks and drivers were going to be needed. Rampaging Elephants wanted to cover events live there and Roberts offered the use of his home and car. He wasn't going to be using them much in the immediate future.

The Free Texas directors came to visit. They discussed the events of the day and likely impact on the opinion of the people of Texas. The next few days would be critical. Having shown massive defiance to the government of the United States, the question in the public mind would be if we were going to get away with it. Every day that Borden County was not occupied by the federal government would cause more people to question the legitimacy of such a powerless entity. The case would be even more compelling if the story could be told of how the people of the county were very happy without the massive amount of government services Washington, DC, and their allies in Austin, thought people needed. Being left alone worked, and it would work even better when applied across Texas.

The place would be crawling with media come morning. Free Texas would hold a press conference at 2 PM tomorrow. They would work out the details in the morning. And there was one more item. Free Texas had been putting together a militia advised by a number of former Army officers, including Roberts. They had just about put together a light infantry battalion. Of most importance to Roberts was the Headquarters Company, that was where they had the people with the support skills and the supporting equipment such as they had, which was desperately needed. The directors decided to activate their militia and deploy it to Borden County. By the time of the press conference tomorrow, they would know if the call was going to be heeded.

Roberts decided to sleep at the gym. If things were calm in the morning, he would get home, shower and shave, and pack some more gear that would be useful for sustained operations. He would also try to see if he could ramp up ammo production at the plant, one problem being that over half the work force for the ammunition plant consisted of militia members. The next fight was likely to result in what the quaint old phrase referred to as "an effusion of blood." And for all of that and what happened today, the best job in the Army was to be a company commander. Soldiers deserved the best commanders that could be found. They kept soldiers alive.

By 11 PM, the first 18 volunteers had arrived.

The morning was calm, and Roberts was able to execute his plan for moving some more gear to the command post.

The county emergency board was there when Roberts returned. They discussed developments. The request from the sheriff for assistance by state military forces was approved by the board and sent off to the Governor. The governor was now going to get put on the spot because he would have to make a decision. He could (A) do nothing and hope the people of Texas did not support the county (B) call out the National Guard to assist the county, which the National Guard Bureau in Washington would probably disapprove and exacerbate the situation (C) send the unarmed State Guard, who might have some tents to bring, or (D) incorporate the Borden County Militia and others into the state military forces. Any of those choices would entail taking political risk, and one or more of the four had to happen. As Roberts explained, the Governor was now in an awkward situation, as well as the US government. Unlike with the IRS agents, there was now no way to pretend that nothing needed to be done at state level.

The other issue was supplies needed for operations and taking donations. They decided the banking system was subject to disruption, so people would be asked to mail donations to the county emergency board, and the board would run the cash via the Freedonia Transaction Company, so at least there was some idea of accountability.

The next item was dealing with the media. Free Texas was having a presser that afternoon, if the emergency board had one too, that would give reporters something to do. They decided to let it run that afternoon, as probably most of the media would be there early afternoon at the soonest, so do the press conference at 2, Free Texas would go at 3, News of the impending tribunal would probably be the lead story and keep the feds off balance.

Next was officers call for the militia, where Roberts laid out the course of action for the tribunal. Roberts would be the convening authority and presiding officer, the XO was appointed defense counsel, and Roy, the first platoon leader would be the prosecutor.

The other two platoon leaders would compose the rest of the panel, having the required minimum number of three as required by the Military Manual for Court Martial. Essentially the tribunal would follow the procedures of an Article 32 Hearing.

Normally, Article 32 hearings were conducted by majors, or officers of higher rank, but Roberts had been appointed to conduct an Article 32 hearing while on active duty as a captain serving in a major's position, and was thus qualified. Later, the Army required JAG officers to be the officers appointed to do Article 32 hearings. Originally the military justice system had been designed to work without military lawyers at all. Roberts had once been requested by an accused solder to represent him as defense counsel. By military tradition, the accused may ask any officer in the Army to defend him, and if it is in any way possible, that officer would be made available for the defense of the accused. It is also widely believed by soldiers that the outcomes of most military legal proceedings are not left to chance.

The XO then went to meet with the accused, and to inform them of his appointment as their defense counsel. He asked if they agreed with the appointment of if they wished other defense counsel to be appointed. He also told them what the tribunal would be like – similar to a civilian Grand Jury, but with the mechanisms of a military Article 32 hearing. There would be a three member panel, a prosecuting officer and a defense officer. This caught ASAC Gallagher's attention. He knew that as a former Infantry officer, the military justice system could be the worst of kangaroo courts, or, in the hands of officers of integrity, much fairer than the civilian system. Gallagher was going to find out right now which it was going to be.

Gallagher asked the XO, "You say we may request counsel?"

The XO replied "That is correct."

"What if we want a Department of Justice lawyer?" Gallagher inquired.

"We will ask the Department of Justice to supply who you want. I would then advise that lawyer on Article 32 procedure." answered the XO.

"What if I want Captain Roberts to defend me?" challenged Gallagher.

"As he is the officer preferring charges, I believe that disqualifies his acting in your defense, in fact he is only the presiding officer as an emergency measure, due to the shortage of qualified officers. If we successfully challenge his impartiality on that basis, he will take on the role of prosecutor." replied the XO.

That told Jack Gallagher two things: (1) These guys showed some pretense to the appearance of fairness, a total kangaroo court wouldn't bother, and (2) he did not want Captain Roberts prosecuting him – in a military setting, even a top notch DoJ lawyer might not get the best of that guy.

SAC Gregory spoke up "We don't recognize the authority of your sham process and demand to be released immediately!"

"The competence of the tribunal will be presented in your defense, but I suggest a hedging strategy would be appropriate. Particularly as the US Congress seems OK with US citizens being tried by tribunals. That is going to work against us." recommended the XO.

"I want a DoJ lawyer familiar with the Uniform Code of Military Justice." Gallagher said "I also want to know what is going to work for us." A substantial percentage of the agents nodded approval.

"I think the only thing that will save you from this tribunal is the Constitution of the United States." And the XO left the internees.

The XO told Roberts of the request for the DoJ lawyer. Roberts said that was expected, and that the sheriff told him earlier that mittens, hop along, and the other two had been sprung by federal judges and were spirited out of the state. The request for the DoJ lawyer would be transmitted to the Red Cross along with the internee list.

There was a great deal of overlap between the county emergency board, and Free Texas, and there was overlap between Free Texas and the militia, so they held a joint meeting to sort out the rest of the day. At the county press conference, that would start off with one of the other members emergency board – the tax assessor, who would promptly turn it over to the sheriff, and then the militia would carry the bulk of that one as they expected most of the questioning to relate to what happened yesterday, and the current situation.

At the Free Texas press conference, they would concentrate on the militia call up sponsored by Free Texas. The logistical support being provided to the militias, is due to the support of Free Texas for an independent Texas, free from federal influence. This would be the setup for the political message which is the foundation for all that had happened. People in Texas want to be left alone to earn a living and raise families. When Texans are not left alone, there will be trouble.

Roberts set out his immediate operational plan. He was going to use the incoming volunteers to do the local security and herd the press into the gym for the press conference setup. The Borden County Militia would wear civilian dress for the rest of the day to perpetuate the stereotype of a bunch of bubbas, as the press will be looking for any kind of visual, and they had to be kept from the internees. It would also mask what the strength of the Borden County Militia was for the next day, which would be an object of curiosity, while hopefully, units would answer the Free Texas call in the next 24 hours. Also, the Roberts property near the ammunition plant would become a militia training and operations base. Only a guard force would remain in Gail for the detainees and some manpower for the sheriff, while the militia buildup would occur farther away from the media glare.

It was now late morning, and more volunteers were arriving, including some from the company Free Texas had built in west Texas. Roberts intended to turn over the guard operation in Gail over to this company as they got to platoon strength, he would fill out the company with the volunteers. The list of internees, 240 taken and the 236 still in custody was emailed, along with the request for the lawyer, was sent via email to the Red Cross, as required by the Geneva Conventions for transmission to the US federal government. Once the Red Cross figured out that this was no joke, and they actually had to do something, that would also be an interesting experience.

The Borden County Emergency Board was not the only entity that decided the events in the county required some action by the Governor of Texas. When the President of the United States is on the line, you answer the call. The two were not friendly and not only because they represented different political parties. They had very different ideas about what the State of Texas should be doing. Neither of the two bothered with the preliminaries.

"Governor, you need to get that situation under control down there. Even if it is a sheriff involved, states can't arrest federal law enforcement. You need to get ready to activate your National Guard."

"Mr. President, that is the second request I've had today to send the Texas National Guard to Borden County. The county wants me to activate the Guard in order to protect them from you." replied the Governor.

The President snapped, "Don't be ridiculous. I want to know what you are going to do about this situation."

"I have a mind to let the legal system run its course." If this situation made the US government more hesitant to push the Texans around, and maybe even more responsive to him, that would be perfectly fine with the Governor. And it was too soon to see how this was playing around the state. The last thing the Governor wanted to do was to take a position that he would have to reverse. It was getting too close to the next election.

"I could send in the Army like Eisenhower did at Little Rock, if you don't move on this." the President reminded the Governor.

The Governor didn't budge "Not sure how many teachers that militia has, but they do have rifles and used them last time. Can you handle another Waco?"

"We could federalize the National Guard. I'm seeing that you are not going to be very helpful in this." retorted the President.

"Mr. President, the way I see it, immediate action is not required. There are Texans who would see sending federal troops as an invasion of Texas, especially when the Texas Legislature has not requested them. And the legislature will not meet for another year, unless I call a special session." concluded the Governor.

That ended the conversation. The Governor decided he needed to have a discussion with that bunch in Borden County to see what this was all about. And the State Adjutant General needed to brief the state leadership on the Texas Military Forces organization and capabilities.

The White House scheduled a meeting in the situation room for 4 PM eastern requiring representatives from Department of Justice, Department of Homeland Security, and the Department of Defense to attend.

By 1 PM, everything was set for Borden County to host the press conferences. The morning crew from Rampaging Elephants had arrived, and was hooking up the sound system. Both press conferences would occur with the Rampaging Elephants banner in the background. The message was being sent that the Rampaging Elephants media outlet was well connected with the goings on in Borden County, and when things got boring reporters started to interview each other. The Rampaging Elephants staff would get some national and international air time when that happened. The staff had arrived by private plane landing on a cleared landing strip, every seat on every scheduled airline flight to Lubbock was booked for the next week. It was certain that some number of people would hear Rampaging Elephants, and a number of them would become listeners. And that number of new listeners was likely to be some number other than zero.

The five US majors, Associated Press, Reuters, and some local Lubbock stations were there from electronic media. Only Texas papers had reporters present. The timing was bad for national print press. They would have to rely on other reporters or be 24 hours behind the news cycle. And those were the papers that everybody in Washington read. Rampaging Elephants was streaming it live on the net.

Sam Voss was first up representing the Emergency Board as the county tax assessor-collector. He was from one of the old families in the county, and said little about the situation, noting only that some assistance for the situation had been requested from Austin. He turned the mic over to the sheriff. Connors stated that he had thought there would be some attempt made to take the IRS agents from his custody, and having been made aware of such a possibility, enlisted the available military forces to keep the peace and the law. As he was not present during the engagement, he would now turn it over to the commander on the scene, who could provide the details he was sure the media would want. "Here is Captain Roberts of the Borden County Militia."

It was now Roberts turn. He gave a summary of the action. The militia had set up a road block, which the federal convoy of vehicles had come across. An armed group of individuals had not properly identified themselves, and complied with the order to ground weapons. A firefight ensued, in which 240 persons were arrested, and those persons now claim to be federal law enforcement officers. The 236 still interred are being held until their status could be determined by a tribunal. Then it was time for questions.

"You said their status needed to be clarified. Is it not clear to you they are federal agents?" asked a reporter.

Roberts replied "That isn't the issue. There is the issue as to whether they had any legal authority to conduct law enforcement activities, and that would be Sheriff Connors remit. The tribunal will be concerned with their status as combatants or non combatants while engaging in conflict against combatants. After that process runs its course, then the civilian legal system takes over. The accused have asked for the Department of Justice to supply counsel, in addition to that provided by us. The tribunal will be convened tomorrow afternoon to give the DoJ counsel time to arrive."

"What gives you the authority to convene tribunals?" asked another reporter.

"The Geneva Conventions require all parties to a conflict to enforce its provisions." stated Roberts.

"You are going to charge the US government with war crimes?" one of the reporters was starting to catch on.

Roberts reminded the reporter "The purpose of the tribunal is to determine the relevant facts."

"How can you charge law enforcement with a Geneva Conventions violation?" a curious reporter wanted to know.

"The Conventions specify that police are non combatants, charged solely with maintaining public order. If they are to take part in conflict as combatants, proper notification to the other parties is required via the Red Cross." explained Roberts.

"Are you claiming that your militia qualifies as combatants under the Geneva Conventions?" the questioning continued.

172

"Yes" said Roberts.

"Are you guys at war with the US government?" one of the reporters thought this was going to get attention.

"The US government seems to be at war with us. We retain the right of self defense." Roberts answered.

"Why should anyone take your secret tribunal seriously?" the reporter's question bordered on snark.

Roberts decided to defuse that immediately "Who said it was secret? And you can cover it yourself and see."

"We can cover the tribunal?" was the surprised reporter's response.

"Yes, if the accused do not request a closed proceeding." Roberts informed him.

"When does the tribunal start?" continued the reporter.

"Tomorrow afternoon, right here." announced Roberts.

Rampaging Elephants got the last question. "Have the people of Texas gotten any help from the Governor or State of Texas?"

"There has so far been no response to our request." Roberts knew that Rampaging Elephants would focus on what was happening in Austin, and that would be a good close to the press conference.

Some of the media took the ten minute break, until the Free Texas press conference, to file initial reports and for quick on scene live reports. From Roberts' perspective, it went well. The focus was on the pending tribunal, and questions about the militia, its strength, capabilities, and future operations had been avoided. He had put the thought out there that the US government had been asked by its agents to provide a lawyer. This would put the feds in a tough spot. If the US government refused to lend legitimacy to the tribunal, by refusing to participate, it would be portrayed as throwing their own people under the bus. A no win situation for them had been created.

Next was the press conference held by Free Texas. As one of the directors, Roberts was there, but did not plan to speak or answer any questions. Ed McMasters was the lead on this one. Free Texas was aiming this conference at the people of Texas and the state government in Austin. Free Texas was supporting the effort of the emergency board and militia as complimentary to the mission of establishing an independent Texas. Many members of Free Texas had moved to Borden County based on the success of many initiatives to reduce government regulation and promote a free market economy and communities based on traditional values of western culture.

For this reason, Free Texas was providing support for the donations requested by the board in terms of money and material. Also, as part of the Free Texas program of Texas self reliance, Free Texas had created its own militia, primarily for use in border security or other needs of Texas. Thus, Free Texas had decided to ask its own militia members to mobilize in order to assist the current efforts of Borden County to repel the federal invasion. Free Texas was urging its members to contact the state government to support the government of Borden County.

"Is this a revolution against the federal government?" asked a reporter.

"No, we are insisting that the US Constitution be strictly obeyed, and Texas should enforce that adherence." McMasters answered.

"What gives you guys the right to form your own militia?" asked another reporter.

"First, we reject the unstated premise of your question. Both US and state Constitutions suppose the whole of the people be armed to provide for the common defense and to enforce those Constitutions. Governments at every level have neglected this obligation, and it has thus devolved to the people themselves to band together for the defense of themselves and the state." stated McMasters.

"But the National Guard is the militia." asserted a reporter.

McMasters had been schooled by Roberts on this point. "No it isn't. First, militia officer appointment is a power reserved to the states, and National Guard officers have federal appointments. Second, the National Guard was founded under the power of Congress to raise and support armies, not the power to arm and organize the militia. See the National Defense Act of 1933, which clarifies this point."

"How big of a militia are you talking about bringing to Borden County?" one of the other reporters wanted to know.

"We have an infantry battalion on the way. That should provide sufficient deterrence for the immediate future. There are also individual volunteers arriving" McMasters stated.

"Why is Free Texas involved in this at all?" one of the Texas newspaper reporters asked.

McMasters played the local angle "We believe in local self government in the context of Texas sovereignty. In the actions of the US government we see a direct threat to our liberty, and it is time for Texas and Texans to enforce their rights."

And then it was time for the set up question from Rampaging Elephants. "How can people help you?"

"We could use cash donations, and equipment donations and the means to do that will be posted on our website." said McMasters.

This press conference did not attract the interest from national news that the previous one did, and most of the reporters were eager to file reports and setup for the evening news, being driven by east coast time. A contributing factor was that they were reporting from a location that had no overnight accommodations or fine restaurants in the county. People submitting expense reports would rather be elsewhere, and Lubbock looked like an oasis in the desert compared to Borden County. For just one example, beer could be had in Lubbock. Their experience would contribute to the reputation of flyover country, and Texas in particular, was inhabited by nothing but ignorant hicks and rubes named Bubba. This perception would be used later by Free Texas.

Meanwhile in Washington, the department representatives were arriving at the Situation Room for the 4 PM meeting. Because of the timing of the meeting, little was seen of the press conferences by the representatives, just the first part of the 2 PM central conference had been seen. DoJ was represented by senior assistants to the Directors, and AG. Homeland Security was all in, with an Undersecretary present, and the TSA Director. The Pentagon was represented by an Army colonel, the tasking being given to the Army, the almost one thousand Army generals on active duty had more pressing duties, and were therefore unable to attend. An assistant to the White House Chief of Staff chaired the meeting.

The first priority was to name the operations group, for reference. The name Texas Rebellion Crisis Working Group was selected after a reasonable amount of discussion. This name should convey the seriousness of the situation and would help shape the public perception that this Texas situation had grave consequences if not handled properly by the government. This would help focus the message to the media sources used by the people in the room. The Army colonel had nothing to contribute, which was fine as nobody wanted to talk to somebody who wears uniforms for a living, anyway.

Next question was the issue of staffing and funding for the group and its activities. The CoS took the action item to see where Office of Management and Budget would allocate funds. Until that was sorted out, the Executive Office of the President contingency funds would be used. While this discussion was underway, the participants were exchanging information on their positions within their respective agencies. The Army colonel turned out to be one of the assistants to the Army part of the operations staff to support the joint operations of the US Northern Command, which supplies military resources to support Homeland Security. At the Pentagon, the buck had not stopped at the lowest level, the colonel had a LTC and two majors that reported to him, but the lowest level of the food chain could be seen from where the colonel was.

Then there was an update on the situation. The plan to have federal judges order the release of the federal agents in the hospitals was successful and the agents were on their way to Washington for debrief to see what information about what had happened could be obtained. FBI and ATF said they did not have much time to lose on

177

this as the agents had caseloads, and if this situation lasted too long, it would cause other investigations and cases to be lost. Agents would have to be reallocated from other offices to cover the shortages. A question arose as to whether the imprisoned agents would be entitled to overtime and compensatory time and how that would be budgeted. The meeting got back on topic.

How was recovery to be achieved? Did DoJ have sufficient resources to mount another operation? The FBI thought doubtful, as about 10% of the agency would have to be dedicated to it. That might work if it could be done quickly, but the number of agents required would probably be well over 1000, and there would need to be a training period before doing the operation could take place. ATF did not have that many agents. Homeland Security dangled some bait. We have Special Response Teams we have been building for taking on highway and rail security in the TSA agency, we could easily make those personnel and equipment available to the operation. This explained the DHS Undersecretary being there, they were looking for something to do and build up TSA further, maybe making this a DHS mission to engage terrorist cells that were active – edging in on this area from FBI jurisdiction.

Maybe we could split this into two smaller operations – get the agents back, and arrest the militia tea baggers later. Or, who knows, at that point maybe the militia would be wiped out in the resulting gun battle. What would the Army do?

The Army was prohibited by law from dealing with the situation. A rebellion would have to be declared by the state government before it became a military issue. In response to the question, yes it would be possible for the Governor to use the state National Guard, using Title 32 funds that would have to be made available

178

to the state. How big of a commitment were we talking here? The colonel told them at least a brigade, and as the Texas National Guard only had two brigades, we were talking half of what Texas had available. By the time they got mobilized and ready for the operation, there might be even more militia there, that would require the second brigade. Given that the militia had already demonstrated an ability to fight, with a competence at least as good as a third rate National Guard unit, a military solution was not recommended.

Except for Homeland Security, most of the group was favoring the Texas National Guard solution. A bigger squeeze was needed on the Governor of Texas.

FBI asked the colonel if there was any background on Roberts. There was. He was a former Army captain – Armor branch who left the Army rather than take a project management procurement job for one of the support branches. It would seem the guy was a fighter, as a retired colonel and retired brigadier general considered Roberts as a potential general. Might have been one too, as he got an award for commanding a brigade during a NATO vs, Warsaw Pact training exercise – he stopped the Soviet invasion in his sector in the wargame. Thus, he was considered a potential brigade commander. Former commanders considered attacking any defense Roberts had planned with time and resources to prepare, to be suicide at worst and extremely bloody at best.

The FBI allowed that as good as he may have been on active duty, all he had was militia now. What did the Army have to say about that?

"You could try sending out 240 agents to arrest him," the colonel suggested.

The colonel would not be returning to further meetings of the Texas Rebellion Crisis Working Group. A suit from the Pentagon would be found who had a better understanding of the Big Picture.

And there was one last item for DoJ. The Red Cross had been in communication with the militia (or should they now be called rebels?) with a request for a DoJ lawyer to represent the agents in a quasi judicial proceeding conducted by the militia. It was decided that calling them rebels would appeal to neo Confederates and might spur copy cat activity, which would not be useful at this time. There would be no question of the US government sending a lawyer to a purported legal proceeding not conducted by a recognized government.

The meeting was adjourned, with little time to plant stories with sympathetic reporters.

For two days in a row, very important public officials in Washington, DC were surprised by events in Borden County, Texas. The evening news was reporting that the failed federal raid had run into the Texas Secession movement which was strong in that part of Texas. As no one in the state government in Austin had taken action against them, the question was being asked if this was part of a state wide secession effort. Additionally, militias in Texas were obviously supporting the Free Texas organization and so far the US government had done nothing. Even more telling was that federal agents were going to be subjected to some militia run legal process. Nobody could stop them. No relevant comment from the President. No relevant comment from the Governor of Texas. There was plenty of comment elsewhere.

Roberts, McMasters, Greenlow, and several other Free Texas supporters, a couple of the Rampaging Elephants staff, and some other militia leaders and friends were watching the evening news and this took on the character of an informal strategy session.

It was time to play on the Texas independence movement full on. Now we can take time to harp on the list of things irritating to Texans that leftist media would not understand. Time had come to bring up the responsibility of the federal government for the lack of border security, pushing homosexual lifestyles on devout people of religion, and any number of other gripes. That might play into the coverage that with the tribunal starting tomorrow, would give the impression that if not legally and politically independent from the federal government, part of Texas was in terms of the facts on the ground independent of federal control.

Roberts was asked how the tribunal played into this. He explained that it served two purposes, one they could get away with doing something that any government in control of its territory would have to do to prevent or lose legitimacy in the eyes of the population. Then the second point is that by conducting a process that would be seen as fundamentally fair and showing the rule of law in action, comparisons would be made between how we conduct government and how the professional political class runs things. Part of our message is to demonstrate in everything we do, that our plan for Texas is better for Texans than what currently exists.

Surely the President was going to react. What would the President do? Roberts thought the President had been put in a tough spot. "If the President does nothing, we win by showing the federal government impotent. If they try to get their people back and fail, then they look even more incompetent. If they use the military to recover them, using the force required to ensure success, they risk civil war or widespread insurgency – this has already gone way beyond Bundy Ranch because now there is a political movement aligned with the defiance of arms. Expect tough talk, but it takes time to plan an operation of any size, and that means at least a week."

The political play was now for the state government. The Governor was waiting to see how the polls and popular opinion went. No Republican can get elected to state wide office in Texas without promising to stand up to the federal government for Texas. It was frequently possible to get elected again without really doing that, but now a tight spot was being created and the Governor was getting shoved into it. Getting this wrong meant the Governor may not get elected again. This was the sensitive pressure point. The fact that nothing had been heard back from Austin indicated that nobody there had a clear indication of which way the wind was blowing.

Roberts commented "Think of it this way – if the federal government can not control Borden County, what chance does the state have? Interesting thought, no? That may have occurred to Austin.

At some time, the Red Cross is going to show up and complain that we are not giving the feds free WiFi and who knows what else. That should play well with our supporters as long as we properly care for them. And we need about $150,000 US in equipment such as tents, cots, clothing, and about $5000 US a day in food to make this operation go. Equipping militia volunteers is going to cost even more. We are going to need either support or a win. If there is another confrontation, I expect there will be serious bloodletting when it happens."

Tomorrow would be the start of the tribunal and more volunteers and militia continued to arrive. The Free Texas battalion would be a key to success. The Headquarters and Headquarters Company would be vital. This was the ability to operate multiple company sized units, integrate people, supply and feed them. Trying to create that from nothing would be brutal. Two volunteers were of special mention, as they were veterans of 2nd Battalion, 7th Cavalry from LZ Albany of November 1965 in Vietnam. One of the two had a son serving in the Borden County Militia.

"My son should have been career Army. He would have been a good soldier." the Trooper remarked to Roberts.

Roberts could honestly say, based on the previous action, "Your son is now an excellent soldier. And he is lucky to have you as his father."

The older vets would be used to run an abbreviated basic training for new volunteers with no prior experience. This would make it easier on the units so they did not have to spend time on the most basic of skills, and could work on unit training.

On entering the gym, Roberts saw that the tribunal was going to get coverage. The Texas Secessionists running Borden County was now a hot news story, and there was nothing else for the media sent to the county to cover.

All of the militia personnel present as tribunal members or as guards, were now in uniform. They wore the old woodland pattern used by the US military from 1981 to 2008. Roberts sat at the table, banged the gavel once, and announced, "This tribunal is convened under the authority of the Third Geneva Convention, Article 5, to determine if persons having committed a belligerent act and having fallen into the hands of the enemy, belong to any of the categories enumerated in Article 4 of the Third Geneva Convention.

In accordance with United States military custom, the tribunal consists of three commissioned officers; a written record of the proceedings; the proceedings shall be open with certain exceptions; persons whose status is to be determined shall be advised of their rights at the beginning of their hearings, allowed to attend all open sessions, allowed to call witnesses if reasonably available, and to question those witnesses called by the Tribunal, and to have a right to testify; and a tribunal shall determine status by a preponderance of evidence.

The accused have the rights guaranteed by the Constitution of the United States and the following rights by international agreement - All persons shall be equal before the courts and tribunals. In the determination of any criminal charge against him, or of his rights and obligations in a suit at law, everyone shall be entitled to a fair and public hearing by a competent, independent and impartial tribunal established by law. The press and the public may be excluded from all or part of a trial for reasons of morals, public order or national security in a democratic society, or when the interest of the private lives of the parties so requires, or to the extent strictly necessary in the opinion of the court in special circumstances where publicity would prejudice the interests of justice; but any judgment rendered in a criminal case or in a suit at law shall be made public except where the interest of juvenile persons otherwise requires or the proceedings concern matrimonial disputes or the guardianship of children.

The Tribunal now asks the accused if the accused wish open or closed proceedings?"

The XO stood and responded, "The accused wish open proceedings." then sat down.

"The prosecution will now read the charge." directed Roberts.

Roy, the first platoon leader stood and read the names of all 240 accused, noting the last four had escaped custody of the tribunal, ending with "did engage in armed conflict, not having status as combatants, with combatants who were identified by a distinctive sign worn at a distance being standard uniforms, were bearing arms openly, were under the command of a person responsible for the actions of his subordinates, and were adhering to the laws and customs of war."

Roberts addressed the defense "The accused will now enter a plea. If the accused refuse to enter a plea, a plea of not guilty will be entered for the accused by the tribunal."

The XO rose and said "The accused challenge the competence of this tribunal under Article 3 of the Third Geneva Convention, Article 3 Section 2 of the United States Constitution, and Amendment VI of the United States Constitution in that requested counsel is not present."

Roberts replied "The tribunal will hear evidence to determine the competence of this tribunal under Article 3 of the Third Geneva Convention, and Article 3, Section 2 of the United States Constitution. The challenge under Amendment VI is not within the power of this Tribunal to resolve, as the presence of requested counsel rests within the power of the United States government, and to the extent it is within the power of this Tribunal, counsel has been provided. This Tribunal stands adjourned until next Thursday afternoon, to allow counsel to submit arguments and time for defense counsel to arrive." And the gavel banged on the desk.

Rampaging Elephants, CNN, and Fox News had carried the tribunal live. Others were probably going to put it on the evening news and there wasn't any other scheduled activity in the county that would give reporters something to do. They would soon have to start interviewing each other. With any luck, the Rampaging Elephants staff would get a number of interviews. That would benefit the cause by getting the message out from people who were obviously well connected with the principals involved in the events.

What became the informal operations group met after the tribunal adjourned. McMasters spoke first. "That was quite a performance, reminded me of the old footage of the Nuremberg trials."

"Exactly what it was designed to do." replied Roberts. "If you were a federal agent, would you have some hesitation about taking a trip to Borden County?"

"I get your point. Where are you going with it?" McMasters asked.

"To establish the point that the Constitution applies to everybody. And if nobody else enforces it, the people themselves will." said Roberts.

They then discussed the status of things in progress. Militia strength had made it up to three companies, the headquarters company was closing in on site, and a fourth company was in the process of organization, and two more companies from Free Texas were on the way. Texas is large, and it takes a full day of travel time for units from east Texas to arrive. With the rate that other volunteers were arriving, they would have seven or eight infantry companies in two days, and would need to form another headquarters company, a battalion staff, and a brigade staff. The shortage of experienced officers was acute.

The first donations were starting to arrive. Money contributions were in the $10 to $20 range for the most part, and larger contributions on occasion. Still not enough and too early to tell if this was going to work. The cash went to food and tentage. By the time the Red Cross showed up, and Roberts was sure they would, he wanted the internees to be under large tentage for housing and have cots for 10 to 20 internees per tent. Next Priority was bedding and toiletries. Porta johns had been donated, which made life a bit easier for the guard force. Somebody sent 500 orange jumpsuits priority overnight. Roberts appreciated the donor's sense of humor and sent a personal note of appreciation.

The militias brought their strength, which was manpower, but also their weaknesses with them. There was almost no unit equipment, and loads of individual civilian tents and camp gear. Hopefully, it would last long enough – either the situation got resolved, or an army would have to be built. There are few entry points into the county by road, Highway 180 and Farm to Market Roads 669 and the 1054 / 1210 junction. Plans were made to have three of the companies control the north, east, and west entry points into the county. This expanded the zone of control to the county border, got the companies some easy operational experience, and provided additional early warning for the guard force and what was now the operations and training center. This would also reinforce the media perception that the county was no longer under the direct control of any other government. The force was under orders only to stop and detain vehicles with US government plates. Word about that would get out on its own.

Two other preparations were made to enhance security of the operation. The call was put out for floodlights to be set around the internment area. In case of a night rescue attempt by unfriendly forces, the floodlights would be used to illuminate the area, and negate night vision devices. The other was an innovation to use motorcycle clubs as scouts across the state looking for vehicles with US government plates or evidence of government activity that might be heading for Borden County. Not all thought it was a good idea to involve the bikers. Roberts said that we are not asking anything of them we are not asking of anyone else, and by going through the umbrella organization for the state, they insulated themselves from any particular group that might be engaged in criminal activities.

As Roberts explained, they were now entering what was known in insurgency theory as the bazaar of violence. Different groups with different goals and agendas will have a transitory commonality of interests, and there will be shifting alliances among a number of groups, each pursuing its own agenda. At this point, it would shortly get to the juncture where Free Texas and the Native Texan Movement would work together on the soon to be political activity. NTM had avoided anything that might resemble a militia, but Roberts expected that they would be very happy with the resulting political situation, even if it had been obtained by methods NTM found unsavory.

There was an item of interest from the White House press briefing that was notable. The question had been asked why the government did not honor the request of the agents held prisoner in Texas for legal counsel. It was an uncomfortable question. Later, the agents union issued a statement critical of the government for abandoning its agents and providing no assistance. If the DoJ did not supply a lawyer, the agents union would.

The Lubbock local Fox News crew found Roberts. He was wanted for an appearance on The Factor that evening. Roberts agreed to the request if the local Fox crew would set it up on location at the gym. This generated additional discussion. The good news was that the Free Texas organization had hit the big time. The bad news was that all involved were likely to be portrayed as delusional separatist loons.

The interview went much as Roberts expected. That was an advantage of having seen the host conduct interviews before. He did the interview seated on a desk dressed out in uniform with gear that looked like the regular army, but in woodland pattern for a slight intimidation effect. It started with the appreciate you showing up and taking the heat line. Roberts responded that when The Factor calls, you do the interview, or you will send Jesse Watters out to hunt you down and then look stupid on national television. That was enough to put the host slightly off balance, and helped with the rest of the interview. The tribunal had as its purpose to establish that the Constitution applied to all, and when the government refuses to obey the Constitution, and the courts fail to restrain government misconduct, the people were in a bad way. That led to extreme measures to put the situation back in order. The strategy was to present a line of reasoning with which the audience would fundamentally agree.

All concerned concluded the interview went as well as could be expected. What was important to Roberts and Free Texas was that their case had been heard by almost four million people in the United States.

Chapter 16

The Governor Wants to See You

It was mid morning when McMasters found Roberts. "I had a phone call earlier this morning. The entire board of Free Texas is to meet with the Governor tomorrow morning. They said to make sure that we did not forget to bring you along."

Roberts found that very interesting. "I would guess that the polling data is in and it doesn't look that bad for us. May I suggest that we keep this under wraps?"

"What's your thinking about that?" McMasters asked.

"We may need to negotiate or make a deal. And if we make a public spectacle of this, we might find ourselves in a position we wish we weren't. Besides, it lets them know that we can be trusted to keep our mouths shut if necessary. That might get them to be more open than they otherwise may be" Roberts suggested.

"Agreed. I'll tell the others." McMasters confirmed.

Roberts told the XO he would be leaving in the afternoon, and would be in Georgetown the next day and then was anticipated to return. He then established the chain of command in his absence, given the arrival of more militia units. He used the Borden County Militia as the strategic reserve. The manpower was being used to set up the training base and ramp up production at the ammunition plant. The idea was to make whoever came after the agents to have to deal with one or two of the other companies before encountering the Borden County company. Even if the others didn't fight, just being in the way would cause some delay, even to a competent commander on the other side.

One of the Free Texas companies was used to cover the east, toward Snyder. One platoon was set along the bridge on 180, another on the FM to Highway 84, which Roberts considered the most likely attack approach. This company had a platoon in reserve. Snyder had a landing strip that could accommodate C-130s, and was on the route to the FBI field office in San Angelo. Another company was set on the west and northwest facing Lamesa with a platoon covering the bridge over 180 and the Colorado River. Another platoon covered the FM intersection in the northwest of the county. The third deployed company covered the FMs to the north, one on the route to Highway 84 on the northeast. Two companies rotated guard duty, the one off being a reserve. There was another company being organized, and was notionally covering the three FMs to the south, each platoon on a FM road at the Colorado River crossings.

The river blocked movement by wheeled vehicles, which meant that whoever wanted to come after them from 260 degrees of the perimeter had to fight for a bridge. Having to do that would confuse a non military organization, who don't train on doing a river crossing under fire. Even a militia unit might be able to hold under those circumstances. The alternative was for the attacker to get out of the vehicles, get wet, and walk over 15 miles to the compound where the internees were held. It would take a military unit to do that. Of course, the military would helicopter in, so there was not much use in heavily patrolling the river.

Next, as the Tribunal would not reconvene for some days the media present would be roaming around the county. This would leave the media without anything to cover for those days, so Roberts thought mischief was likely to result.

The Free Texas Directors packed and decided to car pool to Georgetown. This would give them the chance to discuss matters internally before meeting other Free Texas leadership and the other member of the board in Georgetown, and prepare the messaging for the meeting with the Governor. They had plenty of time to discuss why the Governor might want to see them. After passing through the platoon guarding the east approach on Highway 180, the discussion really got underway. The reason for the meeting could be anything from the request for assistance from the emergency board, although, that would not be a Free Texas meeting, to giving them an ultimatum to let the feds go and give up. Roberts suggested looking at it from the perspective of the Governor.

Roberts told them "By now he has probably had a call from Washington telling him to sort this out, and that means arresting us. This meeting is either the ultimatum to do that, or he is going to tell us he doesn't want to do that, and wants to know what our intentions are and how this ends with no damage done to the Governor. We need to be able to say, what we want, what we are willing to settle for, and what we won't accept. As long as we have 244 captured agents, public opinion, and 1000 armed troops on our side, we have some leverage. While they may threaten armed assault, I'm going to guess at this point it is a bluff unless they feel cornered, or are sure public opinion is on their side."

"What if they arrest us?" Ted Greenlow asked.

Roberts thought "That would be one of the more stupid moves that could be made. That says he is siding with the President and has no intention of living in Texas for the rest of his life."

McMasters asked Roberts why he was sure they were bluffing and what armed conflict would look like. Roberts replied that the use of federal troops, the military, crossed the line in federal law. "The US military can't do law enforcement, and can only suppress a rebellion in a state if the state legislature declares there is a rebellion in the state. You can bet that any number of federal lawyers are at work trying to work around that, probably by declaring the State of Texas is in rebellion. That makes it critical what the state government does. As long as it does not directly cross the feds, they can claim there is no rebellion. That means we also need to be careful on how we present our case.

As for conflict, as long as we can keep the military, and that includes the National Guard to a large degree, sidelined, we will be fine. The FBI has some 10,000 plus field agents, but they don't do military fire and maneuver. It will take military tactics to beat us, but either way, it will be as bloody as our troops are willing to fight. If there is sufficient public support, west Texas is going to become de facto independent – that may be a consideration in the meeting tomorrow." Roberts cautioned.

The rest of the drive was spent in consultation on expanding the membership of Free Texas, how to get better messaging out in the public realm, and most importantly what that messaging should be. Winning support from the people of Texas for what Free Texas had a mind to do would decide their success or failure.

They arrived in Georgetown, and met two of the other board members and several of the county directors on the town square for dinner and conversation. McMasters gave everyone an update on the happenings in Borden County, an especially the value of having created the militia that answered to Free Texas. The county was on the verge of becoming independent, if not in a legal sense, at least in a practical sense. If this message could go Texas wide, it was very likely that other counties in west Texas would follow along. Free Texas may not be the only group of Texans fed up with feds. As things were getting more political, the NTM was also getting some press, and the NTM story matched the Free Texas message well.

Already, Free Texas membership was starting to grow even faster than previously. Texans were giving credit to Free Texas for putting the federal government in its place, and some of the local and state house politicians were making contact about endorsements in the primary election which was just a few months away. Along with the other challenges facing the leaders of Free Texas, rapid organizational growth looked like it was going to be added to the list.

The rest of the meeting was spent reviewing the transition plan to independence that Free Texas had developed. Borden County was most of the way there. It would be the model that Free Texas would point to as the example for the rest of Texas to follow. The goal was to get that message out to the people of Texas. The meeting broke up at 9 PM, and the board headed for the home of one of the board members that lived in Georgetown.

They assigned roles as to which board member should take which part of the conversation with the Governor the next morning. They wanted to play to the individual strengths of each board member.

Most of all, this group wanted to convince the Governor that the current relationship between Texas and the government of the United States could no longer go on as it had for the previous 50 years. The federal government was out of control, and that was no longer going to be tolerated. The Governor could do something about that, or they would.

The next morning as they drove into Austin, Roberts regretted not having had the time to talk to people not already involved with Free Texas. It would be useful to know what people who had found out about events in Borden County from various information sources thought. They got what the military refers to as an intelligence indicator on the way in. Some cars were sporting Texas flags and they saw an occasional Texas Secede bumper sticker. That was unusual for the Austin area, as it was Democratic Party stronghold and loaded with state government employees.

They parked in the parking garage and headed for the Governor's office. As Roberts approached security, he held out his handgun license. One of the oddities of Texas is that most state government buildings have a security express lane for handgun license holders. The Department of Public Safety Trooper told Roberts when you get to the Governor's Office, we will ask you to let us keep that for you. Roberts expected as much, so he was carrying one of his spare 1911s. As they reached the outer office, Roberts was asked for his handgun.

In what Roberts considered a good start to the meeting, he heard a voice from the inner office command "Let him keep it." It is an imperative to be gun friendly in order to be elected to state wide office in Texas. As the Free Texas board members entered the office, they noticed that in addition to the Governor, some other people were present, including the Lt. Governor, the state Adjutant

General, the head of the Department of Public Safety, and some other aides. Introductions were made all the way around.

Then the Governor went straight to business. "I asked you here to find out about your intentions. Or stated differently, which one of you intends to be the next person to sit behind this desk?"

Whether the Governor was joking or not, Roberts decided to make it clear what the limits of Free Texas's intentions were. "Sir, I think you have mistaken us for one of the other organizations." This was a reference to a couple of the Texas secessionist or Texas independence organizations. There was one that insisted it was the legitimate government of Texas, and another one that intended to abolish the state government and take its place. Free Texas wasn't going there. It did not matter to Free Texas who obtained Texas independence, just that is was done. If the current state government did it, so much the better as far as Free Texas was concerned.

That comment did get the Governor to smile. "It would be more difficult to find a resolution to this with someone trying to replace you wouldn't it? So, if you are not trying to replace us, what are you trying to do?"

This was the opening for McMasters to provide an over view of Free Texas as an organization, and that it has a transition plan to take Texas from a state of the United States to an independent republic. This would require transition plans in several areas, starting with a Texas currency, negotiating with the US for allocation of military assets, what would happen to US government entitlement programs in terms of which would cease, and which would be backstopped or guaranteed by Texas. Various border security issues that would arise, and trade policy requiring decisions to be made in areas currently the responsibility of the

196

federal government. And there would be several issues to be negotiated out with the US government to continue trade with the US, and even visa and passport requirements. Essentially it was the case for how Texas could function as a country.

The Governor was only mildly interested in this. "There are a number of groups agitating for an independent Texas, you guys just seem to have given it some serious thought, which does you some credit, but how does what is happening now out in Borden County play into this?"

Now it was Greenlow's turn to describe what had become known as the Free County Project. He gave a short background on Freedonia, starting with the business relocation, and bringing in more of the Free Texas supporters to work the newly created jobs. Then he mentioned the merging of Freedonia with the school board elections, county commissioner elections, sheriff, county attorney, and the impact on electing the judges. In short, the people of Borden County followed state laws and regulations they found useful, and worked around or ignored the rest, including the federal government.

This led to the source of the conflict, and more importantly, Free Texas was in the process of sending the message via the media now present there, that there was very little in the way of government needed or wanted in Borden County. The gentlemen in the room may wish to take heed. They were delivering the type of government the voters of the Texas Republican Party wanted but were not getting from their elected office holders.

Or, to put it even more bluntly, every politician in the room ran on a platform of less government and a willingness to make the federal government adhere to the restrictions of the 10th

Amendment of the US Constitution. That had been delivered to the people of Borden County by Free Texas. How many other Texans would now demand the same thing was the question asked the elected officials in the room. The politicians got the message. It was one thing to run and get elected promising less government, but now there was the real possibility that not delivering on that promise would have political career limiting consequences.

The Lt. Governor entered the conversation. "OK, so you may have gotten away so far with your no government program, and you think that has some relationship to your vision on an independent Texas, but what do you guys want from us?"

Now, it was Roberts turn, "Primarily we want to be left alone. There are things you could do to help us, such as incorporating the militias into the State Military Forces, so we could have access to more resources than we have now. And you could put a referendum measure on the next ballot asking if the people of Texas have had enough of the federal government."

"Isn't that like signing my own death warrant? You are trying to make me into the last Governor of Texas." The Governor commented.

Roberts responded "I think there is a good chance that no matter what you do, you will be the last Governor of Texas. The question is do you want to be the next President of the Republic of Texas."

"You know Roberts, I'm sure you will believe me when I say that I got a call from Washington, suggesting that I use the National Guard to put an end to your operation." rejoined the Governor.

Roberts outlined the situation. "With all due respect sir, you are not going to do that. First, following orders from Washington, would probably do you some political damage that you can't afford. Second, you can't be sure that the Guard will show up in full strength for that sort of operation. Third, we already have two battalions, and are working up to brigade strength. The entire Texas National Guard, assuming everybody shows up, is two brigades, and in order to ensure success, you will need at least three. Fourth, each brigade needs a basic load of approximately 1 million rounds of small arms ammunition, and you don't have any ammo. There is not enough training ammo at Ft. Hood or Ft. Bliss to supply your needs. I own an ammunition plant, and have two million rounds stockpiled for use by our forces. Fifth, we are located far enough away from federal military bases that you will have to establish a refuel point and supply routes to conduct operations that are subject to interdiction and attack."

Apparently, the Governor found some news in Roberts analysis, and turned to the Adjutant General with a questioning look "General?"

The Adjutant General's face flushed. "Sir he is right about the ammunition for one thing, we would have to get it from the Army. And that would take several days."

"Then let's assume the military option is off the table for the present time, that leaves us where Roberts?" the Governor wanted to know.

Roberts suggested "You do have some leverage. If some 244 federal agents somehow got out of our custody, and you were involved in that, it may get you some leverage with Washington. And we could get something out of that."

"Roberts, are you saying that you guys will deal? Had not expected that of you." the Governor became more interested in a solution.

"We did not announce to anyone outside of my chain of command that we are having this meeting. It makes coming to agreement easier." Roberts confirmed.

"Tell me what you have in mind." prompted the Governor.

Roberts proposed "Let's see how this strikes you. The federal agents eventually get bail. You get credit for that. Diffuses the Texas is in rebellion argument. I expect the agents to skip out on bail, and the county will pocket that cash to fund this operation. We don't need trials of federal agents to make our point. We are making it now. The militias become part of the Texas Military Forces. That gives us access to surplus equipment we can use. Politically, this ends up with a call for a special session of the legislature. On the agenda is Texas sovereignty. Result is a referendum for a vote by the citizens of Texas on what they want the state government to do about the federal government. We have refrained from criticism of the state government in this situation so far. This deal puts us on the same side instead of opposing each other." The other Free Texas board members nodded agreement.

"Interesting idea. Have to think about it." said the Governor.

"You guys may survive a primary challenge this time. We will still be there, and probably have more counties with us on the program shortly. We are not going away. In any case, we are working to shift the state Republican Party our way. We will go public with the call for a special session – we have nothing to lose. The more frustration the Tea Party folks experience, the easier it is to convince them that we have a better alternative." Roberts warned.

200

"Gentlemen, thank you for your time, we will be in touch." stated the Governor.

With that, the meting ended, and the Free Texas directors went back to their car. Scholz's Beer Garden was the spot chosen for lunch before heading back to Borden County. Reflecting on the meeting, it seemed a great deal of talk for no concrete result, just a possibility of a referendum. McMasters suggested it was really for the purpose of the political class to feel out what they were dealing with in Free Texas, and what was the agenda that Free Texas was pushing. Being politicians, they were not going to commit to anything before they had to. Roberts saw it as a case of which is the greater fear the office holders have; the campaign financers or primary voters. Until that question was resolved, not much would happen.

On the way back to Borden County, discussion turned to what the special session and referendum might look like. Most of the Free Texas directors were optimistic that Texas was on its way to a course independent of the United States of America. Roberts was not so certain. "The Governor will be sensitive to public opinion from his supporters. He does not want to lose an election. He'll want to remain behind that desk. When he is convinced that supporting us facilitates that, he will move in our direction. The legislature will hose us."

"How so?" wondered McMasters

Roberts reasoned "No Democrat is going to vote for us, so we have lost a third of them right there. We need over 75% of the Republicans to go our way. That will not be easy. We're going to need primary scares and language that comes out of this that is squishy enough to get that level of support."

"We have a good 50% to 60% of the people with us. That's got to have an impact." McMasters was convinced.

Roberts continued "It certainly helps, but the people who finance campaigns will be worried about not being able to do business in the US if Texas leaves, and the propaganda machine in Texas and elsewhere is going to go full tilt on that – it will cost Texans jobs. We have to be able to counter that theme. Along with the loss of government pensions scare tactic as the other big fear. People vote based on fear. We have to make them more afraid to stay subservient to the federal beast."

"Same struggle we have always faced" said McMasters.

Roberts concluded "It is. Some things are different now. We will have more media attention, which is the opportunity to get our message out. We had to struggle to get attention before. And we have one hole card. At least part of Texas is already de facto independent for the most part and doing fine so far. That is an embarrassment to our opponents."

In Washington, the next meeting of the Texas Rebellion Crisis Working Group was underway. They were losing control of the narrative. The Governor of Texas was on the sidelines and had been rumored to have met with rebellion leaders. Scenes from the tribunal played on TV had some impact. About one third of the population supported the federal government, about 40% seemed sympathetic to the rebellion, and 25% had not yet decided which way to go.

The White House decided to send a lawyer to the tribunal to represent the agents. It was hoped the lawyer would be able to expose the whole proceeding as a sham. The interplay between the defense counsel and the lead judge had gained some credibility for the tribunal, and the tea baggers were crowing over the feds getting a dose of their own medicine. With some luck, having a DoJ attorney there might cause the tribunal some problems, and as the FBI pointed out, the attorney could bring back intel from the scene that would be helpful in planning for the future of the crisis.

Putting together any sort of rescue plan was experiencing difficulty. Putting together a force of 1000 agents led to a number of problems looking for solutions. Bringing so many agents together would disrupt thousands of current cases. The only area large enough to assemble such a force would have to be on a military installation, and it would come to the attention of soldiers stationed there. The soldiers would talk. To control and coordinate such a number of agents would require an organizational structure lacking in civilian law enforcement. It was going to take weeks to create such a force and start to train for the task.

Using the National Guard or the military was still the favored solution. This focused attention on the suit from the Pentagon. The suit was sure that military support in terms of facilities, equipment and transportation could be provided. That was as far as the generals would go, according to the DoD suit.

The matter would have to go to the President.

As the directors of Free Texas returned to Borden County, they were greeted by the platoon guarding Highway 180 facing east. Roberts asked if there had been any activity during the day. He was told that just reporters had been around who inquired about the new "border guards", and were left with the impression that Borden County was now guarding its borders from the rest of the United States.

On arriving in Gail, and checking in with the operations center there, Roberts was told that a message had arrived from the American Red Cross. A representative would arrive tomorrow to check on conditions for the internees and that the US Government would be providing counsel for the accused.

The good news is that the request for contributions seemed to be having good effects. Thousands of $10 and $20 contributions had arrived and were being processed. This would keep the existing units fed and somewhat sheltered. The sheer size of the operation was now requiring dozens of people to sustain it. Keeping the effort going was now going to be a challenge of having sufficient money and people. Generals who ignored logistics rarely won wars. Pressure also needed to be kept up on the politicians in Austin. Those politicians had to be convinced that if they did not get on the train soon, they would be left at the train station.

That evening, Roberts approved going ahead with some of the "black" projects. Work began on converting ARs to military M16s and M4s. Additionally, construction began on M240 and M2 machine guns. Some parts had been stockpiled, pending assembly and machining of the receiver part. The same equipment that made the 5.56mm ammunition could also make the 7.62 NATO round for the M240, but was not capable of turning out .50 cal ammunition. That still had to be sourced elsewhere. Two other projects required some engineering effort. Mortar rounds and anti tank weapons were much more complex, but would provide additional capability in case of a serious attack on Borden County.

The Tribunal would reconvene the following day. This would be intended to spark public debate on the role of the federal and state governments by bringing up the idea on whether federal agents were exempt from state laws and the implication of some people not being subject to laws that applied to the average citizen. Roberts doubted that would get live coverage, but should still provide fodder for public discussion. More importantly, this was expected to further agitate the population of Texas.

The next morning, Roberts drove into Gail with the Rampaging Elephants crew along for the ride. Rampaging Elephants was going to cover the Tribunal session live later that afternoon. The crew told Roberts what the media outlets in the county had been doing the previous day. There was getting to be more focus on Freedonia, the militias present in the county, and the idea that Texas might be more than just slightly crazy in that a number of Texans were thinking that they had had more than enough of an oppressive federal government and were supportive of those doing something about that. Some anger was getting directed toward Austin for not being involved and siding with the people of Texas.

Arriving in Gail, Roberts checked in with the militia company on guard duty. A message had arrived from the Red Cross, giving notice that a representative would arrive that day with the US Government supplied counsel for the Tribunal. Roberts expected that it would be late afternoon by the time they arrived. Borden County still generated a great deal of media attention, and flights in or out of Lubbock were booked.

Ed McMasters found Roberts at the school late in the morning, "We have some good news."

"What would that be?" Roberts wanted to know.

"The county emergency board has a response from Austin. We are getting shelter and camp equipment via the State Guard. And there is someone on the way from the State Adjutant General who wants to see you. That isn't all there is, someone from the Governor's office is also on the way." McMasters reported.

"I guess the poll numbers are in and they are favorable for us." Roberts would be curious to see just how much support they were going to get from Austin and if it would be publicly acknowledged that the state now had some involvement in the situation. They would have an idea 24 hours from now Roberts thought.

His train of thought was broken by an unexpected call from Sheriff Connors. "Come over to my office as soon as you can. I have something you will find very interesting."

"I'm just down the street from you. I'll be there in a couple of minutes." Roberts left the school and walked over to the Sheriff's Office.

Sheriff Connors opened the door. "Come on in. I've got a question for you. Are any of your men drug dealers or baby rapers?" By now they had walked back to Connors' office.

"Not to my knowledge. And if I ever found one, there would be repercussions. Why do you ask?" Roberts was very curious.

"I have been inventorying all of the stuff you guys captured from the raid a few days ago. Except for the weapons, ammunition, and radios your people kept. There was a locked case with some interesting contents, specifically about five pounds of cocaine and a couple of USB drives with some kiddie porn. What do you suppose that was doing there?" Sheriff Connors asked.

Roberts speculated "I'd say some insurance to drop on the target of the raid. Did they bring any warrants with them that would tell us who they were after?"

206

"You and I are named on warrants, along with a stack of John Doe warrants that are probably for your men to be picked up. The bad news is that we lost chain of custody on this evidence, the good news is that none of your guys seem to have left fingerprints on the case. Three of your 'internees' did leave prints. None of the three matches are Gregory's in case you might be wondering." Connors said.

"Well, no luck there, but we can be reasonably sure he knew about it. When the time comes to press those three to try and break them, also bring this up to Gallagher. I make him as an honest agent who would spill the beans when confronted with undisputable evidence of corruption. Otherwise, his retirement plans won't include residence in Texas. I assume you are going to the Grand Jury with this?" Roberts asked.

"Absolutely. This is exactly the type of corruption that fully justifies our actions to date. I am determined to increase the state prison population as a result of this. So, whatever you are doing with your tribunal, just remember I want my piece of the action too, so don't let any of them get lost along the way." reminded Connors.

Roberts said "They will be yours in a few days. The Tribunal will not be able to prosecute US citizens. It is really what we call an information operation designed to get people to think about the rule of law, who obeys it, and more importantly, who does not. I hope to make the case to as much of the public as I can, that the rule of law is a central component of western civilization. If they countenance a deviation from the rule of law, their lives are worth nothing to a government with unlimited power."

"It will be a few days before I have the indictments." Connors mentioned.

"I assume we will still have to hold them as there is no room in your inn. How about on the last day of the Tribunal, I make a show of turning them over to your custody, and you can make the news of the indictments known?" suggested Roberts.

"Deal – a pleasure doing business with you. See you later." Connors said.

As Roberts returned to the school, he was met by his First Sergeant. "Sir, you have two visitors. One has a letter from the American Red Cross as the official ICRC representative with himself as the official visitor checking on camp conditions on behalf of the internees. The other purports itself to be a J. Winston Smyth III Esq. from the Department of Justice as chief trial counsel."

"Oh, this is going to be a riot." Roberts had his own company on duty as guards today. "I assume both have managed to make themselves a pain in the ass by now? Please, get the XO to accompany us to the internees, and please have the mess chief provide lunch for the four of us in the office using the officer's mess set. Thanks"

Roberts then went into the office to greet his visitors. He had a late twentysomething man and an older man he guessed to be in his early 60s. "I'm Jim Roberts, the commander of the Borden County Militia."

The younger of the two introduced himself as the representative of the American Red Cross. Roberts figured that this guy's idea of primitive camping consisted of hanging out in the best hotel in the area with other Red Cross relief workers, while any number of people who had just lost their homes and almost everything else they owned were lucky to have a cot in a dry overcrowded tent. Like most US military personnel, he had no use for the American Red Cross. Roberts' uncle had been an infantryman in Europe in World War II, and exhibited absolute hatred the American Red Cross. Based on Roberts' own military experience, he merely loathed the American Red Cross.

Roberts was also interested in the lawyer's story. If they sent someone with military law experience, it must be someone without current court martial time. He figured the lawyer was one of the late 1960s draft dodgers who went to law school and then did two years of military service as a military lawyer to complete his military service obligation. The Boston Brahmin accent was not that of someone who spent two years of his life carrying a rifle. This would be a guy doing a couple of years of "government service" to have contacts in the regulatory environment in order to represent the clients of his law firm before government regulators.

The XO had arrived and he was introduced to the two visitors. "Gentlemen, we will head over to the internees, where the Red Cross can view the camp, be introduced to the internees, and meet their additional defense counsel. We will then return here for lunch, and then you may return to speak with any of the internees without us being present."

With that, the group headed out to the nearest stadium gate. Both officers handed over their side arms to the gate guard, and entered the compound with the visitors. They did a walk through of the tents, each internee having a cot, and a container provided for personal items allowed each internee. The visitors were introduced to Gregory and Gallagher as the representatives of the internees, and were walked out of the compound. Roberts and the XO retrieved their pistols, and escorted the visitors past the guards tents on the way back to the office.

Lunch was served on one of Roberts "acquisitions" - the Outfit Officers Mess Set. There was the main serving tray and two serving bowls laid out with the four plates and table ware, all in GI aluminum. Instead of the coffee pot and cups, can cold drinks completed the setup. Although Roberts had only eaten off such a set once on active duty, he used it on occasion to create the impression that while this might be a militia, it was unlike other militias in the state. The members of this militia knew what a professional military looked like. It would be noted that Roberts was addressed as 'sir' or 'skipper' by the prior service men and frequently as 'captain' by the non prior service members. These men knew what they were about.

The Red Cross representative had the first comments about camp life which went along the line of the accommodations being inadequate and the need for Roberts to provide more adequate climate controlled shelter and suitable recreational and reading materials for the agents.

Roberts replied, "We are aware of our obligations. They are living in tents like the guards. As you will later see as you go back, they get the same food that we do. Any health and welfare items the Red Cross or US government provides will be distributed, except for communications devices. Anything like permanent housing is beyond our capabilities at this time. There is no labor requirement. At worst, we may require them to assist in the construction of facilities for their use. When you go back and do your fund raising appeal for the poor imprisoned agents, I will be amazed if 20% of that actually makes it out here. In summary the internees are kept in living conditions equivalent to that of the guard force, are not subject to public curiosity, and have their legal rights respected as persons under investigation."

The lawyer was addressed next. "Are you familiar with the UCMJ Article 32 process?" Roberts asked.

"I'm former JAG, which is one if the reasons I was selected for this task." Smyth answered.

Roberts gave an over view "In essence, that is what is going on here, so forget federal rules of evidence and all of that. You will get the widest possible latitude to present a defense. Tomorrow will be discussion on the competence of this Tribunal. Nothing about the case itself at this time. It is purely about whether this Tribunal can try them. Any questions about that?"

"I expect to be able to present a rather straightforward argument." said Smyth.

"Indeed you will have that opportunity, just remember that this is not Federal Court." Roberts reminded him.

After lunch was over, the two visitors returned to the internees. This gave Roberts time to see the other visitor of the day from the Governor's office. He was accompanied by an officer from the Office of the State Adjutant General.

"Good afternoon, Major Roberts." The aide greeted Roberts.

"Captain is as high as I got." Roberts reminded him.

The aide the announced "Here is your commission as a Major in the Texas State Guard signed by the Governor. Congratulations on your promotion. Under the circumstances, there is no point in keeping you a captain as you are qualified to be a major in the State Guard. We still had all of your records from your Texas National Guard and federal service."

"Does the field grade lobotomy come with it? State Guard units are unarmed. What orders if any, have you brought with you?" Roberts figured he might as well find out now if it was the intention of Austin to buy him off or otherwise take control of events.

The AGTX officer continued "The Governor is placing you in command of the Texas Military Forces deployed to Borden County at the request of the County Emergency Board. We will set in communications from you to AGTX. The Governor desires that you keep the situation as quiet as possible for the political process to have some impact. I will take back to Austin your recommendations for commissions for qualified officers from the units now present in the county. There will be no public announcement made of these actions. The Governor wants to know what are your intentions."

Roberts reported "The Tribunal will play out in a few days, and barring some unforeseen circumstances, the agents will be released to the Sheriff. He will prefer charges on several things including the fact that they brought items with them for the purposes of framing one or more citizens of Texas for federal crimes. What happens to all of the agents will be a matter for the Texas legal system. I would be very disappointed if someone decided to short circuit that process to the benefit of the accused.

I am interested in enhancing the capabilities of certain units that will now appear to be part of the Texas Military Forces for future contingencies. We will see how these events impact the politics of the state. Is this acceptable to the Governor?"

"I think so. We don't have any budget for your capability enhancement. Please keep it quiet for as long as possible about your integration into the TMF. We are not yet ready to cross that line with Washington." the officer requested.

Roberts agreed "Understood, there is no advantage to us in calling a press conference on any of this. What we do need is the tents, generators and life support that the State Guard would use for a disaster. We also want the ability to buy military equipment via the State at no cost to the State, such as we can not otherwise get. That detail can be worked out later."

"That will be fine. Good luck, Major." the officer said.

The meeting told Roberts how things were going in Austin. It seemed that the meeting with the Governor meant that they had decided that using the stick might not be productive, so they were going to see what they could get with a carrot. Anything given by the Governor could disappear just as quickly. The only thing Roberts really cared about was the ability to acquire more military equipment for the units that might have to either face down more feds or eventually secure a porous border.

One big advantage of being part of the Texas Military Forces was that if things went in their favor, they might eventually be ordered to Texas active duty. That would be a cost to the taxpayers, but the troops would get some pay, and their jobs would be protected. Those were two issues that prevented militias from being as effective as they could be. Deployments were a huge financial drain on the militia members, and people had families to support.

The amount of help to be provided via Austin was the main subject of discussion among the County Emergency Board members. The state government in Austin must have been feeling some heat from the voters in order to get this out of them. How far the Austin politicians were willing to go to really support Borden County was still questionable. At least they were not actively opposing their efforts. That was the good news.

The Board had decided on a 3 PM central press conference daily as the main effort to communicate developments. Today covered two topics – the resumption of the tribunal and promised support for logistical issues from Austin. That was all they had to feed the media for the day.

The tribunal was called to order. The usual media were there, but Roberts guessed that only Rampaging Elephants was going to carry everything live. In any case, the presence of the DoJ lawyer and some probable sound bites should make the major news networks. The gym was full with the accused and reporters.

Roberts opened the proceedings "The Tribunal resumes, and will now hear argument on the competence of this Tribunal. The defense may proceed."

The XO spoke first "Sir, Article III, Section 2 requires trial by jury. The tribunal does not qualify as a jury trial by being composed of too few members, and not requiring a unanimous verdict for conviction. Additionally, as this case arises due to a treaty, the case must be heard by a court authorized by the same section. This tribunal does not meet that criteria. All of the accused are US citizens, and thus must be presented a bill of indictment by a Grand Jury as required by Amendment V." With that said, the XO was seated.

Smyth then addressed the Tribunal. "It is long established precedent that federal officers are immune from state prosecution for acts committed within the reasonable scope of their duties."

Roberts interrupted him. "This is not a state prosecution. A treaty signed by the United States and ratified provides the authority for the Tribunal. You will probably have an opportunity to make that argument elsewhere, but not here."

Smyth went in another direction "The Supreme Court invalidated the original Military Commissions Act for the reasons previously specified."

Roberts addressed Smyth "Now you are on the right track, but this tribunal is not bound by civil precedent. We are taking all issues de novo. And Congress reauthorized the Commissions Act to address those issues."

The XO was back on his feet. "Be that as it may, that Act has not yet been validated."

Roberts than addressed the XO "Well then, good thing for you that we are addressing all issues de novo, or the presumption of validity of a Congressional act would work against you, wouldn't it? Now for the prosecution."

The prosecutor spoke "Sir, it is clear that the Congress intends for Geneva Conventions cases to be handled by military tribunal. There is no example of any war crime being prosecuted in a US

Federal court. All such prosecutions have been conducted by court martial or tribunal."

Roberts took on the prosecutor "But there have not been any such cases. The prosecutions of US citizens were under the "unlawful combatant" theory which is US legal theory and not supported by the Geneva Conventions. And again, we are taking this de novo, the fact that the Supreme Court allows war crime prosecutions of non military US citizens via court martial or tribunal for war crimes does not apply.

Anybody have anything else to add?"

Smyth rose again. "Article 3 of the conventions allows for domestic police activity. Which is the basis of actions of the accused. If you proceed, you will be conducting this tribunal on an equal basis as a tribunal authorized by the President of the United States, which this tribunal is not."

Roberts reminded Smyth "We're not there yet counselor. That will only be an issue if this Tribunal is competent to prosecute. De facto, it is the victors who get to conduct the war crimes trials. If your side wants to conduct the tribunals, it needs to win on the ground."

Smyth thought there should be more, but the tribunal was not using the case law method, but instead using a textual approach to law which negated much of his experience. In reality, the relevant issues had been brought forth and discussed.

Roberts announced "This Tribunal is adjourned until Monday at 1 PM Central Time, when a ruling on the competence of the Tribunal will be made."

While the gym was being emptied, Roberts and the two other judges that composed the tribunal, met in Roberts' office. "Is any discussion wanted before we vote?"

"Sir, I don't think that will be needed, the issues are clear." The other lieutenant nodded agreement.

By military tradition the officer most junior in rank votes first. This is so that his vote will not be influenced by an officer senior to him in rank. Majority vote is sufficient for a decision, except when the death penalty is imposed. A death sentence requires a two thirds vote.

"What is your vote?" Roberts asked.

The oficer said "I vote the tribunal as incompetent. All US citizens not in the actual service of the armed forces accused of a crime, must be tried in a regularly constituted civil court by a jury of citizens."

"What is your vote?" Roberts asked the other officer.

"I vote the tribunal as incompetent for like reasons." He replied.

"And I also vote the tribunal as incompetent for like reasons. I will write the opinion of the tribunal. The decision is unanimous." Roberts declared.

Roberts walked over to Sheriff Connor's office. "Just wanted to let you know that the tribunal will render a decision on Monday about whether or not it can try the accused. How does that work with your Grand Jury?"

"That is fine. I expect indictment tomorrow." Connors said.

"Good. Please be there on Monday should the decision be to turn them over to you." Roberts ask Connors.

"If you do, you will still have to maintain custody because I don't have the jail space. Doesn't really change anything on my end." replied the Sheriff.

"OK, thanks." Roberts left the office.

The tribunal got play on the national press. For the most part it reinforced existing perceptions of what was happening. The hue and cry of the leftist portion of the polity was for immediate government action to crush the rebels. However, it seemed that no one could trouble himself to show up at a military recruiting station and become part of that effort. Risking life to crush the rebellion was something to actually be done by someone else.

On the other side of the political spectrum, coverage was more friendly toward the Texans. The Fox News judicial analyst predicted that it would go in favor of civil court and the agents would not be tried by the tribunal. That was the difference between the current government and the Texans. The Texans demonstrated an awareness of the Constitutional issues.

No matter the politics, the tribunal was being discussed throughout the United States. And the idea was planted that there were some people somewhere that had stood up to the government of the United States and gotten away with it. That was exactly the message that Free Texas wanted to send.

On Friday the Grand jury of the Texas District Court retuned indictments on 240 agents of the US Government, a federal judge and assistant US Attorney for suborning perjury in causing improper search warrants to be issued, and various other charges. The Sheriff also let the information about the attempted frame up be known in order to increase the perception of corruption. That would be great fodder for the Sunday news talk shows on all of the television networks.

So far, it looked like Borden County was fighting the US Government and winning. The major political parties were starting to notice. The party faithful were demanding action. Past that opinions diverged. Free Texas was perfectly happy with that perception of events.

Monday afternoon produced a swarm of media coverage to report the decision of the Tribunal. Roberts dropped the gavel at one minute past 1 PM.

Roberts announced "The Tribunal is resumed to rule on the question as to whether the Tribunal is competent to try the accused. Evidence has been presented by the Defense and Prosecution, and the Tribunal has reached a unanimous decision. It is the opinion of this Tribunal that:

The United States operates upon a hierarchy of laws. In cases where laws conflict, the law taking higher precedence applies, and the law of lower precedence gives way. Therefore we start at the level at which this Tribunal operates.

The Geneva Conventions on land warfare are a series of treaties ratified by the United States with some reservations. The reservations do not apply to this case. Among the provisions of this treaty are two provisions that apply. Every belligerent is responsible for enforcing the Conventions, and every government has the right to prosecute rebellion.

We deal with the provisions thus: (1) As representing combatants under the terms and as acknowledged by the Conventions, this Tribunal has the right to enforce its provisions upon all persons within its power. By falling into our hands, the accused became subject to this jurisdiction. (2) The defense of suppressing a rebellion can only apply to the unlawful resistance to authority. To use this defense, the accused would have to show that their actions were within the scope of The Constitution of the United States, and all laws of the United States. If the Prosecution could show any act by the accused unauthorized by the Constitution of the United States, the defense would fail. This point would only apply if the Tribunal were competent to render judgment on the accused, so it has yet to be decided.

In any case, a treaty made by the United States may not violate any provision of the United States Constitution. This principle is established in Article VI. No treaty, United States law, State Constitution, state law, or any other governmental action at any level of government or office holder may in any way contradict the United States Constitution. This restriction also applies to this Tribunal.

Thus, any right of any citizen or person protected by the United States Constitution must be respected by this Tribunal. Among those rights protected are the right to trial by jury, to answer for an infamous crime only after indictment by a Grand Jury, and as a case arising under a treaty of the United States, trial must take place at such place as Congress has directed by law.

This Tribunal fails to meet all three requirements that must be met in order to prosecute a citizen of the United States for violations of the Geneva Conventions. The interest of justice requires that the accused must have a fair judicial process. While most of the concern about judicial fairness is on the unwarranted conviction of persons not guilty of crimes, a judicial system that deliberately fails to convict the guilty of capital and infamous crimes is equally reprehensible.

For the foregoing reasons, this Tribunal is incompetent to try the accused. The accused are remanded to the Custody of the County Sheriff for disposition.

Is the County Sheriff present?" Roberts asked.

"I am," was Sheriff Connors reply.

"These prisoners are now remanded to you for custody." Roberts said.

Connors now addressed Roberts "In my role as the Sheriff of Borden County, I place you in charge of these prisoners to maintain existing custody, as they have been indicted by the Grand Jury for various crimes, and the county is unable to house them."

"This Tribunal is adjourned." Roberts declared.

Those reporters expecting to hear some justification for a show trial of federal agents were disappointed, and were having difficulty explaining the events. Others were now using the events as an important lesson in what the rule of law really meant. Either way, Borden County was making more news.

Once the realization set in that the agents were still going to be prosecuted in a State court, and Department of Justice attorneys, and a federal judge had been indicted by a state Grand Jury, attention focused on Sheriff Connors.

Chapter 17

Politics is the Continuation of War by Other Means

The Texas Rebellion Crisis Working Group had not been entirely idled by events. The legal staff at DoJ had come up with a plan of initiating legal action against the State of Texas. This was not unusual, but the US Government was going to use a provision in the Constitution to have the case heard directly by the Supreme Court as having original jurisdiction. This would save the time of going through the federal court system. And as there were four guaranteed votes for anything the US government wanted to do, plus voting against the US government would have implications on federal supremacy, DoJ was reasonably certain of success in forcing Texas to free the agents and recognizing the validity of the federal warrants and actions.

In every other case brought before the Supreme Court, states had caved in and acquiesced to federal authority. There was no reason to think that this time would be any different. Anytime some local official failed to obey a federal judge, that official was eventually ground down. As the action had now shifted to the legal system of the State of Texas, that now became the focus of the attack. Until that was resolved, it would be difficult to go after the tea baggers that were the core problem. That became the best ass covering way to present the issue to the President for approval.

As the President had found the Governor of Texas very unhelpful during the entire episode, he approved of the proposal and scheduled a news conference to make the announcement. The President's base supporters were ecstatic. Those Texans that had blocked so many progressive proposals and legislative initiatives were finally going to get what was coming to them. After the Supreme Court smacked down Texas, then real progress could be made. The roadblock had to be removed and federal authority asserted.

Reaction in fly over county was equally passionate. It was clear to these people that the US government no longer recognized any limits to its authority and power. State legislators faced growing pressure to defy federal authority and reign in federal power. Reaction in Texas was the most severe of all.

There had been widespread frustration with the lack of action by the Governor and the rest of the government of Texas by Tea Party Republicans, other conservatives, and some of the previously non political citizens. They demanded action. They wanted Texas to stand up to the federal government. They felt that their fellow Texans in Borden County had not been given sufficient support from the state government, and the current office holders were starting to get filings for challenges in the upcoming primary election.

The Governor of Texas decided that he would make his own announcement about the situation. The action by the President had made it impossible to sit on the fence any longer. The people who voted for him would no longer tolerate inaction. This put enormous pressure on the Republican Party of Texas. More and more of the party members were starting to think of state party officials as being too cozy with Washington, DC.

The date was set for a special session of the legislature of the State of Texas by order of the Governor. The sole item on the agenda for consideration by the legislature was the question of the relationship between the State of Texas and the United States of America.

This action by the Governor only increased the political firestorm. Leftists were calling for military action, some Texans were calling for secession, and mainstream Republicans had the deer in the headlights look about them. Some counties in the Texas panhandle and west Texas were starting to think that Borden County had the right idea, and were also putting pressure on Austin. Locally, employees of the US government were noticing that across the state of Texas and many western and southern states, local officials were being uncooperative. The country seemed ready to split apart and Texas was the focal point.

The situation made political meetings much more interesting to attend.

Membership in Free Texas was expanding rapidly. There were now over 300 local or county groups across the state. The announcement by the Governor prompted a board meeting. McMasters started the ball rolling. "It looks like we are on our way to an independent Texas."

"Yes, we need to be ready for the referendum on the independence vote. At least now we have an organization in place that can really help influence that." Ted Greenlow also felt much more optimistic.

"We have to get seriously to work on our transition plan so we have the answers for how the different facets of an independence Texas will work. There will be some concern about federal programs being discontinued, and we need to be able to soothe those concerns." McMasters was on a roll.

"I think we are assuming too much too soon." Roberts said.

"Why do you say that?" McMasters was taken aback.

Roberts noted "The Governor's call was very ambiguous. It could be a secession convention, or it could end up in a strongly worded letter of disapproval. We have no idea what is going to come out of this."

"We certainly need to influence the outcome." McMasters said.

"That we do" agreed Greenlow.

"Let's look at how we go about that." McMasters got philosophical.

"I'd start with how the ground looks now. There are 150 Representatives and 31 Senators. I'm going to write off the Democrats as going against anything that happens. That gives us about 100 Representatives and 20 Senators that might do something we will find useful. We are going to need 76 votes in the House and in reality all 20 in the Senate. Just one of the Republican Senators could derail the whole deal. This is going to be hard." Roberts had done the math.

"I'm not feeling so good now." was McMasters reaction.

Roberts stuck with his analysis. "This may just be an intermediate step to get us where we need to go. There will be a great deal of inertia to keep things as they are. Too much risk of business disruption, loss of government benefits and other factors. We need to score each of the legislators in Austin and see who we have, who we might get, who we can replace, and who we can't replace. We use this at the litmus test for the next election. For certain, the Speaker of the House and I expect quite possibly, the Lt. Governor will be working against us. Our real job for the Special Session, may be to prevent disaster. We can't risk the failure of a stand up to the feds message."

"I thought we were making progress." Greenlow was now less enthused.

"We are, but there are no shortcuts. We have to form alliances and work the politics of this." Observed Roberts.

"How do you think we get there?" asked McMasters.

Roberts noted "For one thing, the Native Texan Movement has seemed to want to go form a political party for Texas. The time to do that may have arrived. It takes just under 48,000 petition signatures to get a ballot spot. That would be a useful outlet for the frustration that people have. Having the petition drive underway during the Special Session might influence a vote or two. A message could be sent that those who vote the right way will not have a third party challenge. Obviously the focus of that party is going to be Texas independence, so it gives a focal point for action and public policy initiatives to cling to.

The other thing is the message that comes out of the session. I don't see a realistic way we get an independence referendum out of this. We need to push for a referendum on a statement that will appeal to independence supporters while giving cover to a tell the feds off message. If we get a tell the feds off message approved by the voters, we set the stage for the next move. Many of our own people won't like that, but the idea is to move more counties in our direction and state acts to establish Texas control over more of the economy and limit federal influence. Provide more real freedom, and then the politics will follow, just like in Borden County.

Then use the resulting frustration to target the politicians who are too soft on this. The blame can be put on the politicians who say that this is all we could get. I just don't know yet if they are more afraid of us or their donor base. For now, I'm going to assume they are not that afraid of us. They will try to find some way to hose us."

"Makes sense to me." agreed Greenlow

"Me too" said McMasters

"Agreed" Gene Smith had entered the conversation as the fourth of the Free Texas Directors.

Roberts continued "It gives our members something positive to do where the results are largely within our span of control. With luck we will peel off some Republicans and some of the other groups can be rolled into the effort. The message is simple for the ambitious ones, once the party is formed, then we can have the food fight over who runs it. But at least most of us should agree that this will move all of our goals forward."

"After all of this, if we can't get 50,000 signatures, there is no hope for Texas." McMasters suggested.

The next day, Free Texas sent out a press release telling the world that Free Texas was sponsoring the formation of the Lone Star Party. The party would be a Texas only political party focusing on running candidates at the county and state level. After formation, the party members would hold a convention to write a party platform. Every petition signer would be a party member and eligible to hold party office and vote for representatives to attend the convention. The initial party organizers stated their intention to push for a law that no election could be won with less than 50% of the vote. The third party splits the vote argument was going to be taken on as the first order of business.

The state leadership of the Republican Party of Texas was in panic mode. At the state level, elections in Texas were straight forward, The Republican candidate took 57% to 67% of the vote. The Democratic candidate took 30% to 40% of the vote. The same proportion applied to the distribution of Senate and House seats. One third of the seats were held by the Democrats and some two thirds held by the Republicans. That pattern had been stable since Texas flipped toward the Republicans. A new political party in Texas was unlikely to take much strength from the Democratic Party.

The bulk of the Lone Star Party would come from the Republican Party of Texas. There was no doubt about that, but how much loss would Republicans suffer? That was the unknown and the problem. If the Lone Star Party got 10% of the vote or less, Republicans could still win. Anything over 10% could be fatal to the Republican Party. Could the Lone Star Party take away 20% of the Republican votes? That is all it would take to put Democrats in power in Texas. Would the Lone Star Party take the risk of Texas being controlled by Democrats? The Republican Party would have to play on that fear. How sensitive would the office holders be to pressure from the Lone Star Party? There were more questions than answers.

Meanwhile, the Lone Star Party decided to play offense. In addition to the petition drive to obtain a ballot line for the party, there were other initiatives under way. The Lone Star Party wanted to work with the Republicans to have a run off system by which every office holder had to get at least 50% of the vote to take office. This proposal was designed to prevent three way races and let people vote for the candidate they preferred, with the assurance that if a candidate did not get a majority of the vote, the top candidates would face another election and the process would continue until one candidate won a majority of the vote. If the Republicans could be convinced that if they did not support such a system, they would lose elections, enough of them would agree to put the system in place.

The Lone Star Party intended to appeal to people who had not been involved in politics, in addition to peeling off the Republicans who had been ignored by their own party. There were a substantial percentage of people who did not vote in elections. While it was probably true that some did not care to vote, the assumption by the Lone Star Party was that many people did not vote because they thought voting was pointless and served no purpose. Those people now had an option to send a message to the two established parties. The real goal was to force a run off election against the Republicans and Democrats. While it was unlikely that the Lone Star Party would take Democratic House seats, they might get a Senate seat from them and more importantly, get enough seats from the Republicans to force coalitions.

Coalitions would be to the advantage of the Lone Star Party. If the Republicans allied with the Democrats to keep the Lone Star party frozen out, more Republican supporters would be driven away to the benefit of the Lone Star Party. If the Republicans allied with the Lone Star Party, the initiatives of the Lone Star Party being enacted would be the price of the alliance. If a few Republican very conservative office holders switched to the Lone Star Party because of the treatment they had received from the Republican Speaker of the House and his allies, this would be another bonus for the Lone Star Party.

Evaluating the House, the Lone Star Party looked at what changes might be possible. They figured the 52 Democrats will be fairly solid, the number might be reduced to 48 with some fortunate events. Lone Star might get two of those seats. The 98 Republicans were going to be where the action would be. If they lost more than 22, the Republicans would have to make a deal in order to keep the Speaker's chair. Lone Star figured the deal would be made with the Democrats to punish defecting Republicans - both office holders and voters. Such backstabbing might make the Republicans the third largest party in the state after the intervening election.

The Senate was the larger problem for the Lone Star Party. At most, there appeared to be four sympathetic Senators out of the 31, and only 15 would be up for election in the next cycle. This is where the push back against the federal government would be sent to die. It could take a couple of elections before the Lone Star Party would be able to influence the Senate. To get there faster would require events to occur that the Lone Star Party could not influence. The Democrats would likely retain their 10 seats, so Lone Star had to get six seats to force coalition building.

All of that was in the future, as the task at hand was to create the party and try to influence the special session. While the objective of the Free Texas organization was to get a referendum before the people of Texas to decide on Texas Independence, tasks had to be accomplished in order to make that happen. Nobody knew what would come out from the special session, but most of the Free Texas board realized it was a long shot. The Free Texas strategy was the main topic of discussion at a board meeting.

"We have to get everybody behind the referendum on the ballot – we know the Democrats won't do it, so the push will be on the Republicans." Ed McMasters was ready to go.

"Do we have the TEA Party groups on board with this?" asked Ted Greenlow.

"I've spoken to some, and they are all for standing up to the feds." said Gene Smith

"That is not the same as the referendum." Ed noted.

"We also have to get the petition drive done for the party. That will scare them." Smith mentioned.

"Do we have relationships now with any of the Representatives or Senators?" Greenlow inquired.

"I think only through the TEA Party groups" Smith answered.

"Jim, you haven't said anything. That is not lake you." Noted McMasters

"Never really cared for politics, it isn't the sort of thing that I like to deal with very much." replied Roberts.

"Why don't you humor us and give a summary of where you think we are?" Smith was curious about Roberts' opinion.

Roberts said "I see the special session as the relief valve to give the public the idea that somebody in Austin is doing something in order to deflect the anger at Austin for not doing anything. The petition drive is critical, if we can get it turned in about a week after the session opens, it will get publicity and keep the heat on. We will know that if we have the signatures at turn in, so we can go ahead with the formation of the party, and hope the Secretary of State makes the announcement that we have a qualified party while the session is still underway. That will add to the fear factor of just what we may be able to do.

The other parties nay or may not talk to us at that point. If they do, we might be able to influence what comes out of the session by influencing who may or may not have a tough election challenge next year. Our promise in that regard will be just as good as theirs – meaning worthless. What comes out of the session will either be some meaningless resolution, or if we can swing it, a referendum with language that is vague enough to get independence supporters to vote for it as well as those mad at the feds but not yet ready to break away from the US to vote for it.

That is our 'compromise' with the established power brokers to show we can play at this level. Meanwhile we put the party organization in place to make it possible for the good Republicans to jump to us while trying to get election law changed to require more than 50% to win an election. With enough fear, the Republicans may go for that, especially if they have less than 76 seats after the next election. We may get there with enough people mad at the legislature for doing nothing in the special session but producing a piece of paper.

That should set the stage for us to win some seats. Then we can work with the remaining Republicans to elect a new Speaker, and move some of our agenda through. When we start cutting back on entitlements and property tax revenue, Democrat supporters may decide to move somewhere else, and people who like the Freedonia model may decide Texas is for them. That program should grow our power base. Something is actually changing and for the better.

And we still have a group of militias that serve as a reminder that there is a great deal on non political power out there. We are ignored at great risk, that some may get bored with politics and opt for a more efficient solution. That is a powerful message. We are the people who will get this done by whatever means necessary. The voters who have been ignored for a long time might respond to that."

"Not a bad analysis for somebody that doesn't do politics. Let's work that plan." Smith suggested.

Freedonia was in the midst of an economic boom. The influx of militia units and media had placed a number of people in contact with the settlement. Freedonia had also gotten some interest stories as background material as news reports. There were more than a few people who liked the idea of living there. Freedonia had no traffic signs or speed limits. There was no zoning to tell you what to do with your property. There were no police, just an armed citizenry. Your children could play outside by themselves without being stolen by Child Protective Services or perverts. It was the life many Texans remembered from their youth, and the life they wanted their children to have.

All 760 lots in the town had been sold and Freedonia was having a construction boom. Some 200 houses of various descriptions from portable buildings, to mobile homes, to slab foundation were under construction. This had raised some $800,000 in FRNs, or as Freedonians thought of it, just over $50,000 in real money for the water system and streets. The initial investor in the tract of land pocketed just over $25,000 in real money profit as the last lots to sell got a bit expensive because there were several interested buyers. He was ready to do this type of development again. He and by now other investors were looking for more nearby land to buy, or maybe export the scheme to the neighboring county.

The Freedonia Transaction Company was also prospering. A number of new accounts had been opened. Those people who were worried about the state of the economy could deposit their precious metals in the new safe deposit box section, open an account, or trade in their US coin junk silver for Promissory Notes as a convenience. Whatever the future might bring, people knew there was one financial institution in Texas that would not have assets seized by the US Government and your deposits were safe. The Freedonia Transaction Company offered mortgages for property in Freedonia at 1.25% interest for the 15 year and 1.5% for a 30 year term. Deposits paid 1% interest.

More people around town meant more business. Three more sections of store fronts were under construction. Some small businessmen found a place where federal regulations did not apply to be attractive for business. One small business man noticed that by ignoring EPA regulations on the construction of gasoline storage tanks, the cost of building a convenience store was cut in half. No retail chain could compete with him because the corporate lawyers would not sanction taking the risk of not complying with government regulations.

The looming increase in population meant that it was very probable that a school would need to be built in Freedonia in addition to the two churches under construction. That would also bring a few more jobs into the community. The sales tax revenue would fund town needs. Some thought was given to the power situation. The development made the residents think about their relationship with the power cooperative and measures needed to assure a reliable supply. Maybe Freedonia would need its own municipal power utility, just as it had a water utility.

As well as things were going in Freedonia, there was one problem they could not solve on their own. Freedonians, like all Texans, were subject to property taxes.

Still holding the agents had a tremendous impact on the militia situation. Sheriff Connors expected that soon, the appeal on the refusal of bail would be heard, and the agents would be granted bail.

As Connors told Roberts, "It is unusual. We are really just holding them because we have a good reason to think that they will not appear for trial based on the four that got other sheriffs to obey a federal judge."

Roberts understood "That really doesn't worry me. From my perspective, they have lost much of their military value as prisoners. At most they have hostage value to prevent another raid or military action. I'm just not into hostage taking."

Connors continued "Of course the Constitution is pretty clear about giving the accused bail, and it is exceptional not to grant bail in a non capital crime."

Roberts considered the implications. "Part of me says not to object to bail as long as it is set high. When they don't show, the county gets money to pay for this mess when the bonds are forfeited. That could be millions."

Connors noted "Save us the cost of a trial, too. But there would be over 250 fugitives from justice working for the federal government."

"I suspect the true number is quite a bit higher than 250." observed Roberts.

"What do you think the county should do with the money?" asked Connors.

Roberts suggested "Pay off county bonds, lower property tax, pay the school district for use of facilities – they are probably close to having to build a school in Freedonia. If it was a $250,000 bond on each agent that gets forfeited, that would be $62 million for the county. Might be able to afford to get some militia gear as well"

"Never thought of this as a money making operation" said Connors

"Unfortunately, you have colleagues that do" remarked Roberts.

"I'm looking forward to having nothing to do again" said Connors.

Roberts joked "Don't bet your paycheck on that."

"What do you think is going to happen next?" Connors asked.

"I don't know. But it seems there is always someone, somewhere, intent on doing something stupid, and can't be deterred from it." observed Roberts.

Connors agreed "That is the story of a lawman."

The people of the United States are a generous population. Just over $500.000 had been contributed to the operation by people all over who had been heartened to see that finally, someone had stood up to government abuse and put a stop to it. The money had been in actuality contributed to Free Texas. Some money was still coming in daily. $100,000 had already been spent and allocated for operations to date and the next week. Roberts was asked about what to do with the rest of the funds.

Roberts suggested doing two things. Take half and use it to by unit gear for militias – field kitchen capability, communications gear and tents. That would let units sustain themselves on an extended operation. That capability was missing in most units. With the other half he suggested building a camp at a training area for militia use. The regulars and National Guard had use of the military installations with ranges, training facilities, and troop cantonment areas. Militias had none of that available and quality of training suffered as a result.

If they ever got to serious fund raising, another conflict point with the government would soon be reached. Once they set about to procure automatic weapons, mortars, and artillery, there would be other issues. As a now state sponsored militia, the federal restriction on who was permitted to have those items should no longer apply. Roberts was certain that if the federal government was asked for approval for the Borden County Militia to purchase those items, the entire unit would die of old age before the Department of Defense and the Bureau of Alcohol Tobacco and Firearms signed anything.

The rule that only state sponsored militias could have those weapons only applied as long as no state sponsored militias could afford those weapons. This was going to be an issue because militias had now become popular in Texas. New units were being formed all over the sate. Free Texas was providing all of the help it could in the form of advice and coordination with existing militias. It seemed there was only so much militia the State Adjutant General could handle. It was never considered that thousands of Texans would be willing to pick up a rifle and defend liberty. The feeling had always been there under the surface. It just needed an incident to cause the spark to flame.

The Governor, Lt. Governor, and Speaker of the House met in the Governor's office. As they were all members of the Republican Party, the meeting was friendly.

"What have you got in mind for the Special Session?" the Speaker asked the Governor.

"I'm looking for a resolution condemning federal overstepping of the 10th Amendment or a resolution to sue the US in the Supreme Court. Something like that to appeal to the base." was the Governor's response.

"They are pretty irate out there. I'm sure you see what has been coming in for calls and email." said the Lt. Governor.

"This will let them blow off steam now, so it gets released before the primary." suggested the Speaker.

"What about those liberty caucus types, who knows what they will introduce. One of them might even want to secede?" noted the Lt. Governor.

"We have enough votes to kill that. Won't even need the Democrats for that. The 10 that are retiring don't have to worry about how they vote – we just need to take care of them." said the Speaker.

"Make sure it doesn't get out of control. That is why we are taking this on now, before the next election cycle. We have to show some action in order to cut this off before we end up with a Lone Star Party." the Governor remarked.

"I wouldn't worry about that. The last time some Texas independence group tried it, they got maybe 15,000 signatures. That will get nowhere." assured the Speaker.

"We have to keep the Republicans in the fold. If a Democrat ever wins state wide office, we are through." Cautioned the Lt. Governor.

"At the end of the day, they will vote Republican. They have nowhere else to go." the Speaker was confident.

"You need to make sure it stays that way." said the Governor.

The following Monday, the Special Session of the Texas Legislature was gaveled into session at 1:30 PM. The usual opening session bloviating took place along with the procedural items such as organizing the House into a Committee of the Whole. These labors fatigued the legislature to a degree that required adjourning by 3:30 PM. One of the advantages to a special session is that the politicians are gathered in the same geography for campaign contributors. This facilitates the smooth exchange of information between legislators and those who require the services of government. Everyone figured the first week would be nothing but various addresses and introducing any resolution or bill that might relate to the relationship between the State of Texas and the US Government. The message from the Governor had been so ambiguously worded that it would take several days to introduce measures, rule on their consideration and amendments. In summary, the whole procedure was designed to accomplish nothing.

During the week, the Texas Court of Appeals ruled on the emergency appeal submitted by the US Department of Justice. US agents, now being held in Texas confinement by the Sheriff of Borden County, were entitled to be released on bail. Public reaction tended to be very unfavorable, and the Texas legislature in Austin was a convenient target for this displeasure. In a twist to the story, not a single bail bondsman could be found to provide the $300,000 bond set for each agent. The risk of losing the money was too great to be tolerated. The Department of Justice could either leave the agents in jail, or deposit $74.4 million with Borden County to ensure the appearance of the agents in court.

A lawyer from the Department of Justice walked into the office of the Clerk of the Supreme Court of the United States and left a stack of paper with the Clerk. The first line on the first page of the stack of paper read: THE UNITED STATES v TEXAS. The Attorney General of the United States then held a press conference to announce that the US Government had filed suit against the State of Texas for interfering with agents of the US Government in the performance of their office. This was picked up in the conservative press as feds claim immunity from state laws.

This action met with widespread approval among supporters of the Democratic Party. It got the opposite reaction from about 60% of the country and 75% of Texans. Perhaps this time, the US

240

Government had gone a bridge too far for most of the people of the US. Fortunately for the people of Texas, the Texas legislature was in session on this very topic.

Relations between the Republican Party leadership in the Texas Legislature and the Democrats had been very cordial. Most of the Democrats had voted for the current Republican Speaker of the House, and some Democrats actually chaired committees in the House. It was now poison for a Republican to be seen with a Democrat. Republicans in Texas were acting like Republicans in Washington, and the Republican voters had more than enough of that.

The petition drive for the Lone Star Party was going well, and Free Texas decided to do a partial turn in on Friday. A press conference was scheduled at the steps of the Capitol to announce the start of turn in. Free Texas was turning in approximately 120,000 signatures of the less than 48,000 needed, and would continue to collect more petitions. Free Texas was also holding a rally on Saturday and all Texans were invited. Free Texas was pushing the event hard in order to send a message to the Austin political class. Not said publicly was that meetings between Free Texas, some TEA Party groups and a few of the more conservative Republican office holders had already taken place.

Many organizations conduct rallies at the Capitol in order to get attention. A small rally attracts about 60 people, 200 is about average attendance, and 500 would be a huge rally by Austin standards. By 2 PM on Saturday, Free Texas had over 5000 people crowding the grounds, Rampaging Elephants supplied the sound system and was covering the event live. Television was there as well. The rally made national news.

For years being a member of the Texas House or Senate was fun. People wanted government to do things and would gladly pay for the privilege of having the state send money or power their way. Suddenly, it wasn't fun anymore. Too many people were wanting the federal government out of their lives. They were past tired of having government dispense largess on those who contributed to political campaigns.

On Monday, 10 Republican House members and one Senator announced that they were switching party affiliation from Republican to Lone Star. The Republicans now had 88 House seats and needed to keep 76 to maintain control. West Texas county level office holders were soon following along and switching to the Lone Star Party as well. The political class talking heads were now openly discussing if the Lone Star Party would have between 30 and 40 seats in the next elections.

The Governor, Lt. Governor, and Speaker of the House though it prudent to hold another strategy session.

"This is getting out of control." the Governor observed.

"We are still OK in the Senate." said the Lt. Governor.

"We have to save the House. It is in real danger of falling apart there." was the assessment of the Governor.

"The Democrats will still support me for Speaker. There is no way the Democrats would ever form a coalition with Lone Star" reassured the Speaker.

"Something is going to have to come from the session that will calm them down. We need to find out what it is going to take to do that." concluded the Governor.

"Isn't that the problem, nobody can tell who is in charge over there and can make a deal." observed the Lt. Governor.

"Who do we have that is still on reasonably good terms with the defectors?" asked the Governor.

"May need to talk with some of the power brokers in Free Texas as well, The ones behind the whole Lone Star Party thing. If they are going to run people for state wide office, we need to know that." remarked the Lt. Governor.

"I think we can set that up." offered the Speaker.

The Free Texas and soon to be Lone Star Party brain trust was holding its meeting in Georgetown.

McMasters greeted one of the Republican House members switching to the Lone Star Party. "I can't tell you enough how thrilled we are to have you switch to the Lone Stat Party. We will do everything we can to get you reelected. Like we said before, any primary challenge will be strongly discouraged, We need you to be ready for the general election."

"Speaking for myself, it is about restoring liberty for the people of Texas. I'm not afraid of a fight." the Representative said.

"What do you think our chances are?" asked McMasters.

"There are a number of retirements, so those races could be free for alls. If a good TEA Party winner does not emerge, then the primary winner could face Lone Star in November. We should have a good chance to so some good." said Gene Smith.

"What is going to happen in the special session?" Greenlow asked.

"Good question. It was designed as a do nothing, but being sued by the feds in the Supreme Court changes the dynamic." Thought Roberts.

"What can come out of this? Independence?" Ed was back on focus.

"Not yet. The votes are not there and no chance in the Senate." The Representative said.

"Can we get anything out of it?" Ed wanted to know.

"Maybe a resolution or referendum." the Representative confirmed.

"Let's go down the referendum path for a moment. Can we sell an approach that says there are a bunch of angry people out there and a referendum diverts attention to a vote and away from the legislature. Would that sell with the RINOs?" asked Roberts.

"Depends on the language and the idea of it being non binding would be a plus." said the Representative.

Smith remarked "For strategic reasons, I like the idea of it being non binding. We can't afford a failure at this juncture. It also lets us be for it while sending the message it does not go far enough. That is also going to be a fight inside the party over the platform. We have those who want Texas independence yesterday, and we need to appeal to those not yet ready for independence."

"That is why I hate politics." Roberts said.

"We have to be able to have a negotiating position. We want a referendum. Then we work out the language of that referendum." Smith proposed.

"Agreed?" Roberts asked.

It was agreed that the party position pending the convention and platform being adopted was that the question should be put to the people of Texas.

After having conducted a statistically valid sampling of petition signatures, the Texas Secretary of State determined that the Lone Star Party had submitted enough qualifying signatures to be a recognized political party in the State of Texas.

"We can stop gathering signatures now, and move on to the next step" McMasters observed.

As Representatives of a recognized political party in Texas, the Lone Star members formed their own caucus, and elected a leader. It was no surprise that the leader of the Lone Star caucus would be a Representative that had voted against the current Speaker and had every legislative initiative of his shut down by the Speaker's allies.

The Speaker meets from time to time with the caucus leaders. The meeting between the Speaker and the Leader of the Lone Star caucus was not going to be cordial, but it was civil. It was the position of the Lone Star Party that whatever came out of the special session should be put to the people of Texas as a referendum. As to whether there was any specific proposal or statement that had to be included in the referendum, the Lone Star caucus was flexible as long as the right of Texas to limit egregious federal actions was included.

This message was relayed to the Governor and Lt. Governor. A referendum would be expensive to run on its own, maybe it could be combined with other elections or if necessary, avoided if everything could get by on a pure Republican vote. Trying to crush the Lone Star Party before it got going made sense, but it entailed risk. It was better to check with the party operatives.

The Republican Party was losing support. The money donors were still there, but the people who did the work as volunteers were not there. They were moving to the party that got results. If the Republicans were going to get those people back, they had to appeal to the voters desire to see some action. The primary was not far away and the ground game was looking bad for the country club Republicans. They decided to co-opt rather than crush the Lone Star Party. Accommodation had been made with the Democrats, why not the Lone Star Party too. Keep knocking them down to 10% of the vote by taking on their issues and as they are not well financed anyway, they would wither away. After all, this was just a slightly more strident TEA party.

The Republican Party would deliver a referendum to the people of Texas.

Republican pollsters went to work to see what language would appeal to the Republican voter and be acceptable to party donors and supporters. Word went back to the Lone Star caucus that a referendum was acceptable. The Republican members of the House would work up the language and after passing the House, the matter would be taken up by the Senate.

This news was communicated back to the Lone Star Party organizers. They decided to call Roberts with the good news. While Roberts was a member of the board of Free Texas, he did not play a role in the Lone Star Party. When asked why he wanted no role in the Lone Star Party, Roberts had stated that he would rather go skiing in Switzerland. For whatever reason, Roberts did not play an official role in the Lone Star Party.

Roberts response to the good news about the referendum was "They are looking for a way to screw us."

":How so?" asked Gene Smith.

Roberts surmised "One way would be to put our guys in a position to vote against what comes out. It could have some really stupid language. At least we have only committed to the position that the people should vote on it. As long as we keep our distance, that position will serve us well. We can always claim it's not good enough and the next legislature should do better than that after the election."

"OK we'll be careful" Smith said.

Roberts reminded Smith "Don't forget that those guys are at war with us. They do what they do for a reason."

Smith noted "They could also schedule the referendum with the primary to drive up party vote and we won't know the referendum results until it is too late to have an impact on the Republican primary."

":That would be my guess." said Roberts.

"So we just try to avoid the crossfire on this? People expect us to do something." remarked Smith.

"Our message is that we have delivered a referendum that other wise would not have happened. If there were enough of us it would have been a meaningful referendum." McMasters broke in.

"Then the message is instead of elect more Republicans, elect more Lone Stars? Asked Smith.

"Why not? Look how well it has worked so far." Mcmasters noted.

"But we are supposed to be the guys who are different." said Smith.

"Forming a political party like the other guys is not doing something different. It makes us more like them. That is something to keep in mind." interjected Roberts.

"What do you suggest we do?" asked Smith.

Roberts suggested "Behind the scenes push for the referendum with the language about the relationship between Texas and the US. We want them to keep coming back to us to check on the language. When it comes to the floor, see if it has enough votes to pass. If it will pass without us, vote present."

"But we promised them that we would support it in the House. I can't break a promise." Smith maintained.

"We said we would support it, didn't say we would vote for it." observed Roberts.

"Aren't you sure that you are not really Bill Clinton wearing a Jim Roberts mask?" Smith joked.

"That is politics. It just shows them that we can play it as well as they can." Roberts said.

"Dirty pool." McMasters noted.

"So it is." Roberts agreed.

With any luck, the Republican Party of Texas would discover how well the Lone Star Party could play Austin games as well as, if not better than it did. It was hoped that such an action would leave an impression on their minds that would not be forgotten.

Chapter 18

Referendum

Eventually, a proposal by one of the House Republicans became the call for a referendum to be presented to the voters of Texas. As expected the Democrat members voted against it, the Republicans voted for it, and the Lone Star members surprised observers by voting present. The Speaker was furious and headed straight for the leader of the Lone Star caucus.

"We just said we wanted a referendum and we would not oppose the language. We never promised you that we would vote for it." the Lone Star caucus leader told the Speaker.

The Speaker was taken aback, which was unusual for him.

"We can play the game, too." observed the caucus leader.

"Can't tell what will happen in the Senate." Warned the Speaker.

The caucus leader was prepared "Too late – you now own it. Let me be clear, we are going to urge the people of Texas to vote for it as weak as it is. The Senate can pass it as is, or tinker with it and send it back to the House to try and put us in a tough spot. Do that and our message will be that a Republican controlled House and Senate can't even get one simple thing done without screwing it up. That is why Texas needs us."

The Lone Star Party and by extension, Free Texas had appealed to an under appreciated undercurrent in Texas. Constant government tinkering with people's lives was messing up their future.

Almost every cattle rancher is a member of the Texas and Southwestern Cattle Raisers Association. They have 25 special rangers (who are commissioned peace officers by the Texas Department of Public Safety) who do nothing but deal with livestock theft and other ranch related property losses. Their relationship with the US Government is not a happy one. As Texas has become more urban, policies adopted in Austin have had adverse impacts on them as well. Their various self insurance programs have been impacted by Obamacare, the IRS, and state property tax legislation. Add on layers of government red tape from the EPA, Department of Agriculture, and Department of the Interior with the BLM, and this produces a leaking keg of gunpowder.

Ranching is a way of life in rural Texas. Large ranches are legendary. The King Ranch is larger than the state of Rhode Island. At one time, it got into a financial squeeze, and borrowed money from the even larger George Ranch. While these operations represent enormous wealth, the cash flow is wildly variable, and at any given time, the cash position could be tight. A rancher who is not careful with his assets and cash will not be long in business. Ranchers expect the same degree of fiscal care from their government. Where ranching rules, Texas county government is in effect, the entity that coordinates services between ranches. Enter the property tax. State law requires a county appraisal district to value (using state required guidelines and certifications) the property in the county. Valuations are based on market value or agricultural use. Based on location, the valuations can be wildly different, and thus taxes for market value property can easily triple, or go even higher if the tax assessor changes valuation method or value of the property.

Depending on how the property owners want to operate, valuations are kept as low as possible, with a higher tax rate, or valuations at a reasonable value and a low tax rate. In either case, a rural county usually ends up with a couple of million dollars in tax revenue, whether it needs it or not. School districts have a state mandated minimum rate for property tax. If a district raises too much money per student, the "extra" money is taken by the state and given to other "poor" school districts. Counties with $500 million to $750 million in property value and less than 500 students have "extra" money.

When an organization such as Free Texas shows up in certain places in Texas and talks about changing that system and eliminating the influence of the federal government on your business, it finds people willing to listen. A number of county officials in Texas counties located north of Interstate 20, and west of Interstate 35 took interest in the Lone Star Party. Many county office holders in these counties were considering changing parties from Republican to Lone Star in the primary election a few months away. They knew that they were going to win the election, so party label was not that important in terms of winning or losing an election. But it was a way to send a message to Austin.

The organization of the Lone Star Party was designed to build on rural Texas as its base. Every county in Texas had the right to send one delegate to the party convention. Decisions were made by majority vote of the delegates. A county with population over 500,000 people was authorized one additional delegate based on that population. A county with a population of over one million, was authorized an additional delegate, and so on. Bexar County

(San Antonio) and Tarrant County by this method had four delegates. Collin, Denton, El Paso, Fort Bend, and Hidalgo County were to have two delegates to the convention. Travis County got three delegates. Dallas County was allocated five delegates. Harris County, which is where Houston was located, would therefore have nine delegates to the Lone Star Party convention, and could thus be outvoted by 10 rural counties. A maximum of 269 delegates would conduct the first Lone Star Party convention. The 37 high population county delegates would not be able to outvote the over 200 low population county delegates.

This reflected the devolution strategy of the Lone Star Party that a county should govern itself. If the central problem in US politics was policies being decided at the federal level and being forced on the states that did not like them, replicating the same system at the state level made little sense. As the 18th Century political philosopher Montesquieu noted, the larger the territory governed, the more tyrannical the government.

While the Texas Senate was cogitating about the language to be submitted to the people of Texas on a referendum, the Lone Star Party was selecting county delegates. Many of the delegates were Free Texas County Directors. This represented the close ties between Free Texas and the Lone Star Party. In the larger counties it was common to see one or more delegates also from the Native Texan Movement or even a Republican with a following that had crossed over to the Lone Star Party. Borden County was unique in that three of the Free Texas Board members lived there. Roberts took himself immediately out of consideration.

"I hate politics. People spend three days debating about whether to say 'happy' or 'glad'. It drives me nuts." Roberts declared.

"There will also be election for the Party Chair and the 25 member Lone Star Executive Board. You will end up on the Board anyway." McMasters predicted.

Roberts announced "If nominated I will not run, and if elected, I will not serve. You may remember that quote from somewhere. By inclination, I'm a soldier. We make it a practice not to do politics."

"There have been exceptions." Smith noted.

"And probably more of them have been bad than good in the long run. Washington was certainly an exception, but he was not career military, contrary to his wishes." rejoined Roberts.

Smith added "Neither are you, contrary to your wishes. There needs to be some way to make use of people we need as advisors. Doing it under the table is crap as a policy and is how the parties do it now. I want something different for us."

Roberts was conciliatory "Agree Perhaps something like this could work. The Lone Star Party is going to have a platform. Many of those planks will relate to public policy areas. One idea would be to have a committee of five or seven delegates come up with the proposed plank. In doing so, they may rely on a group of five advisors, approved by the delegates. That makes it so the who is involved process transparent. At the end of the convention see what had worked well and modify based on experience. There is no reason the Lone Star Party should be run like the others, and success probably depends on doing things differently."

"That is why you should be on the Board." stated McMasters.

"It would interfere with my skiing in Switzerland." said Roberts

In Austin, the Republican Party decided there was nothing more that could be accomplished via the Special Session that would help tamp down the anger and reduce support of the Lone Star Party. The referendum would be voted out, and the Republicans could concentrate on the impending primary elections. The people of the Stare of Texas would be asked to vote on the following proposition:

'The Stare of Texas should take immediate steps to preserve its sovereignty against illegal acts by the Government of the United States'

That was as far as the Republican Party could go. Texas played a large role in the Republican Party at the national level, and no risk could be taken that would harm the chances of Republicans winning national office. Even this language had raised a howl among the Democrats. The national press was branding Republicans as secessionists trying to bring the Confederacy back from the dead. A number of Republicans had seen this language as too risky.

The Republicans and Democrats in Texas could at least get back to the business of running for office and raising money from contributors who needed the government to do something for them. It was something they understood how to do. It was necessary to raise as much money as possible in order to stamp out the Lone Star Party before it got itself established. Republicans and Democrats agree on many things. One of the areas of agreement is that the people of Texas already had all the political parties they needed, and no more political parties are required.

Nobody could figure out what the language meant. Was Texas going to defend itself in the court case at the Supreme Court? Was

Texas going to start its own legal action? Was the Governor going to call out the State Guard, militia and take over the Texas National Guard? Was anybody actually going to do anything? The Governor said he was waiting on the decision of the people of Texas. But what were the people of Texas going to decide?

The Lone Star Party announced that it would hold its first state convention in Brownwood, Texas at the Brownwood Coliseum. The national media that cared, and most of the metropolitan media in Texas had to google the search term 'brownwood texas' to find out where Brownwood was on a map. The tourism slogan of Brownwood is 'feels like home' and for some 200 of the delegates of the Lone Star Party, a town with a population of less than 25,000 certainly would. Roberts and the Borden County Militia would provide the security for the convention.

The convention was scheduled to start on a Saturday. National media relied on local affiliates to cover anything of note that happened. There were no major hotel chains and Michelin one star restaurants to attract reporters from New York. Some group of fools thinking that they could start a political party wasn't news anyway, but there might be some amusing footage or a quote or two to be had. That would be good for a laugh at Texas on a slow news day.

Most of the delegates arrived on Friday and checked in to one of the three larger motels. None of the motels had facilities large enough to host socializing for all of the delegates and alternates, so the evening get togethers would be at the coliseum as well as the convention activities. Friday evening would be the first chance for many of the delegates to meet each other, and also their first opportunity to meet prospective party board members or potential party chair. As he expected, Roberts himself was an object of curiosity. Meeting members of the Borden County Militia was also something that several delegates wanted to do. To see and meet the men who had stood up to the federal government and beaten them was something the Free Texas members and party organizers thought would impress the delegates. It would also send a subtle message not to waste the efforts of those who made the Lone Star Party possible

When asked why he wasn't running for a party office, Roberts could then steer the conversation toward those he thought would be good board members and the person he though best qualified to be the chair. While Roberts hated politics that did not mean that he wasn't capable of practicing it. A couple of ex Republicans and one of the Native Texan Movement guys were working the delegates hard for the party chair position. Elections are always a challenge for a republican form of government. All it takes is for one election to go wrong and the consequences are devastating. Like Churchill said – it was the worst political system ever devised, except for all of the others.

Rampaging Elephants was there to cover the convention live. This was a huge moment for the founder and the station's staff. They saw this as a major event that lead to more liberty for Texans if not Texas being on the way to independence. They were going to come away from the convention with weeks of material. Like with Free Texas and the militias, relationship between the Lone Star Party and Rampaging Elephants was destined to be a good one. They did a number of interviews with office holders who had switched to the Lone Star Party, or who were going to announce the switch at the convention

By the opening of the convection at 10 AM on Saturday morning, 250 of the 254 counties in Texas were represented. Four of the low population counties, such as the 56 voters in Loving County, did not yet have a party member, or one able to make the journey. Ed McMasters of Free Texas served as the temporary chair. The first order of business was the certification of the delegates. Roberts reported 265 delegates present, thus requiring 133 votes for election. 127 alternate delegates were present who were authorized to attend all sessions where delegates were present, but could only vote if a voting delegate was absent. The delegates voted to accept Roberts report, and he was discharged from the credentialing task. Roberts thought to himself, "And thus ends my political career."

The next item on the agenda was to elect the permanent chair of the party for a two year non repeating term of office. Four nominations were made. The two ex Republicans and the Native Texan Movement guys who had been working the room Friday night, and one of the Free Texas board members. The delegates prepared to vote. The 265 paper ballots were printed off, and each voting delegate lined up to be handed one ballot. The delegates went into a curtained off voting area, and deposited their paper ballots in a ballot box. The ballot box was then brought on stage, opened and McMasters counted the votes, announcing each ballot, so the votes could be tallied.

Gene Smith, the other board member of Free Texas, was elected as the first chair of the Lone Star Party of Texas, with 171 votes. Smith was called forward, and handed the gavel by McMasters. Roberts was happy with the result. Smith had been a major influence in getting Free Texas moving, realizing the importance of having a real plan and thought out public policy behind the movement's objectives. There was also something else about Smith that Roberts thought made him the perfect first chair of the Lone Star Party. Gene Smith was not a citizen and did not have the right to vote in Texas. Smith was a New Zealander, he was a legal immigrant, and had been trying to become a citizen for years, his case tied up in Immigration and Naturalization Service red tape for those years. That someone who loved Texas so much could not fully participate in shaping its future was a disgrace.

Smith was the poster child for everything wrong with the US immigration system. As a successful businessman, he would be just the type of person happy in Texas. He was just what Texas wanted, someone who would invest in the economy and grow a business, employing people and creating jobs. Obviously, INS didn't know how to deal with such people. If the process to legally immigrate to the US and become a citizen took less than 20 years, it was considered a miracle. As the Lone Star Party was going to take a hard line on illegal immigration and the resulting costs to Texas of such uncontrolled chaos, a party headed by a non citizen immigrant would quickly torpedo the Lone Star Party hates immigrants rhetoric.

The next task was to elect the executive board. The board would select from among its members a vice chair, to act in place of the chair if the chair was absent. The board would also be the disciplinary organ of the party. The board would certify primary results for party primaries, and delegate choice and credentialing. The board would also propose bylaws and amendments for ratification by the delegates.

There were less than 50 nominations for the 25 positions. Roberts noted that about 20 of the nominations came from the high population counties. The ballot process took considerably longer than the first vote. The good news was that 17 of the 25 positions had been filled. Ten of the 17 were from Free Texas. The Lone Star Party had decided for the most part to dance with the one that brung them. Two of the ten Free Texas members now on the executive board were Ted Greenlow who was the Borden County Delegate, and Ed McMasters who was the alternate. Greenlow handed the Borden County Delegate badge to Roberts.

"Tag, you're it."

"Unfair, now I'm going to have to vote on all this stuff."

"Democracy in action. Ed and I voted, you lose."

"Indeed, you lose is how democracy tends to work."

In the next round of balloting, more than a few delegates noticed that Roberts was now wearing the Borden County badge and was participating as a voting delegate. Roberts himself could appreciate the irony. One of the things he had liked about Free Texas, and the same was happening in the Lone Star Party, was if you really wanted a leadership position, trying too hard to get it would disqualify you. The culture of the organization encouraged demonstrated ability as the grounds for advancement and discouraged ambition. Roberts hoped that would last.

That next round of voting brought the number of elected board members to 23. There would be one more round of voting for the last two seats. The method of dropping the bottom 49% of the candidates helped to consolidate votes quickly around a second choice if the first choice did not make it to the next round. The last two seats were filled and the convention broke for lunch.

The morning host of rampaging Elephants went straight for Roberts. "I'm here at the Lone Star party convention with Jim Roberts, who as you know is the militia leader that finally stood up to the federal government and put a stop to some of their unconstitutional activity. Are you satisfied with the activity so far?"

"I think it has turned out very well, we have the best possible choice as Party Chair in my view. The executive board is a good representation of the people who have worked so long and so hard to give Texans another option to the political class that have gotten us into this mess." Roberts answered.

"In previous statements to myself and others, you said that you were not running for any Lone Star Party office, and yet here you are now as the delegate for Borden County, Your comments Jim Roberts." Was the next question from the radio host.

"I am being held against my will." replied Roberts.

"What can we expect in the afternoon session?"

"Probably some proposals to start to structure the party, and of course there will be the party platform.

"Thank you Jim Roberts."

Roberts had several invitations for lunch. He accepted one from a group of delegates from the Panhandle. He had not worked with any of these people in Free Texas, by the time they had joined, Roberts was in Borden County and the board was meeting with county groups in the state by video conference. As useful as that was, it was not the same as meeting in person. The morning host of Rampaging Elephants was invited along as well, being a party member and supporter.

The topic at lunch was the total uselessness of the referendum language and whether it was worth the bother. Roberts was in favor of supporting the yes vote effort. His reasoning was that if you want something to really get done, then the message is to vote for us. Why they should vote for us should be clear from the party platform, so getting that right was important. If this weak language referendum fails, we have to go into spin mode saying it failed because it wasn't strong enough. All of the national media won't accept that. If it passes, we get to complain it wasn't enough and vote for us because we will really do what our platform says. That second message is the easier one for people to believe.

One of the things that Roberts had liked about Free Texas and the now the Lone Star Party was that he was dealing with the good people of Texas. These were the people he remembered as a child in a small town in Texas. These were the people who were the backbone of America, the Army, and the gun rights movement. They were the small and family owned business people he dealt with when doing some political activism. They were the people you wish you had for your neighbors, the people who looked out for each other and helped each other out anyway they could.

Whoever said that you couldn't go back home again wasn't from Texas.

The convention was called to order for the afternoon session. The first motion to be considered was one from the old provisional chair on the subject of delegate allocation. The current allocation was one delegate per county and one additional delegate for every 500,000 population. The proposal was to amend 500,000 to read 250,000. This would produce more delegates than the currently authorized 269 by some 40 delegates. The debate method for the party was to have two lecterns on the stage, one labeled FOR and the other AGAINST. Delegates who wished to speak lined up behind the lectern, and speakers alternated with a maximum of five minutes each. When debate was done, the chair asked who was for, and delegates held up their badges, he then asked who was against, and delegates held up their badges. If it was too close to call, the paper ballot was used.

The proposal got much less debate than Roberts thought is would. Rural Texans had been trampled on by the cities for years, and now that it had been stopped in the Lone Star Party, he thought the rural counties would be hesitant to let in an increase in urban representation. In this case the previous votes had been so dominated by the rural counties that it got no resistance. It probably helped that almost everybody who met at the convention got along well and the ambitious ex Republicans had been easily checked. One of the FOR speakers remarked that even with the additional delegates, the rural counties would still have a more than 2 to 1 advantage. The motion passed easily. The question was raised as to when the change took effect. The chair asked for a vote of immediately or at the next convention. The decision was in favor of immediately, and Roberts was tasked of providing delegate credentials to the now qualified delegates. With those present, the required vote total now increased to 150 to pass.

The next item on the agenda was Lone Star Party support for the referendum. This got delegates to their feet, and the line on the AGAINST side being the longer one. The delegates took turns giving their reasons on why they concluded one way or the other. After about 20 minutes of debate, Roberts rose, and many delegates took notice as he walked over to the FOR line. A few delegates ahead of him decided to vacate their places in line, and then a few more. A couple of the AGAINST delegated in line then took their seats, and then a few more. In slightly longer than two minutes, Roberts was the next speaker. The delegate speaking AGAINST finished and Roberts was next.

Roberts advanced to the microphone, "Thank you Mr. Chairman. The delegates here today have given many good and valid reasons why this referendum is an empty gesture and useless exercise. Why should we waste our time and energy on it? As hollow of a statement of intentions as it is, it serves one useful purpose. The people of Texas can voice their desires. Are they unwilling to have more and more of their freedoms taken away by what purports to be lawful authority. If the referendum passes, we then have the opportunity to press on and make the case to the people of Texas that not enough has been done, and our Party should be given the opportunity to do more. If it fails, we may have lost an opportunity to move forward toward our ends without the sacrifice of much blood and treasure. Who will bear that risk?"

That ended debate. It was widely assumed that Roberts was speaking not just for himself, but for the hundreds that had taken that risk of their blood being spilled. Where Roberts led, a sizeable part of the militia would go. Soldiers followed officers who won battles. The chair called for a vote. The show of badges was too close to call. The paper ballots were printed. The ballot box was carried to the stage and the ballots counted. The Lone Star Party decided to support the referendum by a vote of 164 to 135. The chair called for a 30 minute recess and the delegates approved the call by the chair.

During the break, several delegates approached Roberts. Most of the conversations were along the line of I felt I had to vote against supporting the referendum, but nothing against you, I had to vote my conscience. We've had enough and you are the only one to do anything about it. Hated to vote against you, but I can't vote for anything that won't solve the problem. Roberts replied that he understood. He was for the referendum for strategic political reasons, and that is why politics stank. That was also why Roberts hated politics. There was nothing personal in it at all. It was also an important point about the Lone Star Party going forward. Disagreements were being managed civilly.

After the break, the Chair started in with the Lone Star Party platform. There were a number of proposals. If the delegates agreed with the objective of the proposed plank, a committee of five to seven delegates would be appointed to develop the plank for the party platform. The committee would be able to consult with a panel of up to five experts who were not party delegates to assist in developing the plank for adoption at the next convention. Smith was going to start with the easy ones first, and work toward the more controversial.

The first party principle to be considered was abolition of the property tax. There should be an amendment to the Texas Constitution prohibiting taxes on property. The line FOR was long and there was no opposing line. The Chair asked if the delegates wish to proceed to the vote, the show of badges was massive. The show of badges in favor of the principle seemed unanimous, there were none opposed.

The next party principle to be considered was border security. Should the Lone Star Party support a military solution to prevent unauthorized border crossing. This drew several speakers. The speakers stated why they were totally dissatisfied with the current approach by the state government of using the DPS to essentially do more of the INS catch and release program. Illegal aliens were to be kept out of Texas as an absolute uncompromising principle. The vote on this was unanimous as well.

The next principle for discussion was toll roads and use of gas tax money. The delegates were fed up with tollway authorities and their use of eminent domain to build roll roads. The party principle was that toll roads should be unconstitutional. Nobody voted against that principle either.

The next principle brought forward were some of the government reduction proposals. One was to eliminate the State Board of Occupation Licensing and Regulation. Does one need a license from the State of Texas to be a florist, hair dresser, barber, air conditioner repairman, electrician, and any other trade or occupation? The delegates of the Lone Star Party thought not. They also thought Child Protective Services and welfare programs to be unnecessary. If you need help, your church should be able to help take care of you. .

The last principle to be brought up for discussion on Saturday was the Lone Star Party discipline principle. Each candidate for office running as a Lone Star Party candidate, was expected to agree in writing with the Lone Star Party platform. If a Lone Star Party office holder voted against legislation that conformed to the Lone Star Party platform, the executive board would have the power to ban that office holder from the Lone Star Party ballot. The Lone Stat Party had more than enough of electing politicians who broke campaign promises. In the Lone Star Party, there could be a faster way of fixing that problem than the next primary election. The banned candidate could appeal to the voting delegates at the next convention. The delegates voted to have the executive board formulate such a policy to be approved by the delegates for inclusion into the party bylaws.

The Saturday session adjourned shortly before 6 PM.

Some of the Free Texas members and Rampaging Elephants hosts went out to dinner.

266

"We sure have come a long way in the past 18 months. It is like I can see my dreams being realized." Ed Mcmasters could see the light at the end of the tunnel.

"Sure we got some breaks, but a great deal of hard work and sacrifice have gone into this." Smith agreed.

"There is still a long way to go." reminded Greenlow.

"True, but I can see the progress. For so long it seemed that nothing was happening and then, boom here we are." said the morning host from Rampaging Elephants

"Long term trends in history are much more obvious after they happen" noted Roberts

"Amplify on that, Jim." asked the owner of Rampaging Elephants.

Roberts went into lecture mode. "Texas has a complex social fabric as a result of its history. Foreigners not from Texas – no offense intended to those not born here – may never pick up on it. It is why Texas may have an Anglo minority and still be a very Republican state and the leftists never figure out why. They can't see past the racial demographics to the people of Texas.

The first Europeans in Texas were the Spanish. But it was the outcasts from power in Mexico City and the adventurous that went to Texas. While the priests were trying to bring western civilization to the natives, the others were acquiring that fierce independence that matched well with the first Anglo settlers. It was that combination that led to Mexican independence from Spain and then Texas independence from Mexico, when Mexico became a dictatorship.

Those Tejanos and Texians shared a common bond. A love of the land, and a love of independence that hard work and isolation from a government far away, much like with Great Britain and the 13 colonies. It changed toward the end of the Texas Revolution when the first set of carpet baggers arrived from the United States. They knew a victory would mean that vast tracts of land and a great deal of wealth would then be possible. And it was. But they brought that fast road to wealth attitude and slaves with them. So many came, that they ended up controlling the Republic of Texas, and treated many of the Tejanos like Mexican peasants. Even some of the heroes of the Texas Revolution felt compelled to leave Texas for Mexico.

Be that as it may, the dream of Texas survived. Texas offered a fresh start for those who needed it. It didn't matter who you were or where you came from. What mattered was who you are now and what you became. As a state, the population of Texas grew rapidly. Just like many of its people, Texas started over in 1865. But that also brought the next load of carpet baggers from the United States. The Tejanos became foreigners in their own country, and while the Indians were being eradicated, the state became run by men beholden to Washington.

The push back started in the 1880s, and the wealth of Texas shifted from cotton to cattle. In a sense the ex Confederates were real Texans. When a fight breaks out, they don't ask why a fight broke out, they ask which side are we taking. They took the side against a government that had not respected the wishes of the people. Too much of that push back was directed at the perceived benefactors of the men Washington sent. Unfortunately that push back also took the form of the Klan.

Over the next 50 years, the cattle boom became the oil boom. Anybody willing to work hard could prosper. The Texas myth was grounded in reality. In the 1970s we started to get our last group of carpet baggers - government bureaucrats. The other carpet baggers could be partially escaped from by going to the frontier, but these can't.

For all of that, the myth of Texas remains because it is based on fact. Did you notice that in what might be thought of as Democratic counties, our delegates are Tejanos? The glue that held what the leftists think of as the Hispanic demographic is really held together by Tejanos. When you see the name John Martinez or Nancy Ramirez, those are Tejanos, proud Texans who love Texas like any of us, Christians who have strong family ties, and in many cases cousins in Mexico. They are no different than us – they believe in hard work and independence and are fiercely proud Texans. Just like us, they will offer a hand up, but not a hand out. That is how the Republicans got 30% of the "Hispanic" vote in Texas. It is the Tejanos who are the backbone of the community, who thanks to an overbearing government, have to contend with Democratic Party carpet baggers intent on ruining their communities, too.

The soul of Texas is immortal and can never die. It is a part of us who are Texans. Some Alamo visitors are shocked to see it in the middle of downtown San Antonio with a street running through the grounds, the fortress compound containing commercial buildings, and the fact that it was almost torn down. Even if the Alamo was destroyed, it would still live on in each of us. That heritage of defiance to tyranny is ours. The belief in our own abilities and Texas as a land of opportunity is ours. The myth that the American dream found its ultimate expression in Texas is our legend. As long as we live so does Texas.

For all of that there is one oddity. For too many Texans the myth of Texas is enough. As long as the myth is there, they don't worry about the reality of Texas. That is how we reached the point at which we had to act.

We have been successful, because we speak to the soul of Texans wherever they may be." Roberts concluded the lecture.

"You need to write that down." said the owner of Rampaging Elephants.

"I was a bit concerned on that referendum vote. We almost left our House members hanging." remarked McMasters.

"I wasn't sure it was going to pass either, when I called for the paper ballots. Turned out to be close but made it." noted Gene Smith.

"A few votes may have changed when it became a secret ballot. You have more flexibility in private than you do in public when everyone is watching." observed Roberts.

"Which brings us back to the current situation. So you think the independence principle will make it tomorrow?" asked the Rampaging Elephants host.

Roberts responded "I'm doubtful. It may be a bridge too far for many of the Lone Star members who came directly from the Republicans without making a stop first at Free Texas. It will take them a bit more time to come to the realization that there are problems in the US that we can't fix. They are ready for nullification, but not secession"

"Hope springs eternal doesn't it? The reality is that there is a 90% chance that one leads to the other." Smith predicted.

"Yes, but I can't see any shortcuts." Said Greenlow.

After dinner, they walked back to the coliseum where the Lone Star Party was having its party. The media that had been covering the convention got all the material needed to convince the rest of the United States and the World that the Lone Star Party was full of crazy Texans, as if there was any other kind of Texan. Most of the attendees viewed the situation as about 500 good folks having a good time and some annoying reporters. Roberts played the part of one of the mini celebrities along with the office holders who had switched party affiliation. It confirmed in Roberts' mind, that one of the five worst things that could happen to you in life was to become famous.

The next day at the convention, things moved more slowly. The sound money principle made it through. If Texas started to mint its own silver dollars, that would be one more chain that stretched to Washington that could be broken. Same with the call for a reform in election law to require 50% plus one to win. That would be a major benefit to a small party trying to win seats. The two big parties tried to scare voters out of voting for any other candidates via the fear that the worst candidate would win if the voter voted for the best candidate.

School finance was a tough one. The property tax was the primary means of funding schools. When you have a platform of no property taxes, there has to be some other solution for schools. Increasing the sales tax to 10% seemed to be the most widely supported alternative, combined with school choice. Considered opinion was that federal mandates would have to go away for any of this to work.

The delegates worked through the list of principles. The last one would be the toughest.

The chair brought up the principle that Texas should be an independent republic. Almost every delegate headed for one line or the other. Many delegates used their full five minutes to speak. Roberts hoped that soon everybody would realize there was not anything to add to the topic. The Chair soon came to the conclusion that the principle was not going to be adopted, so he set about trying to create a substitute. The principle that Texas should nullify unconstitutional federal laws gained traction. The independence supporters got added to the platform principle, the call for the elimination of unconstitutional federal departments, meaning those that did not exist in 1789. More importantly, was the principle that employees of the US Government inside the borders of Texas are subject to the laws of Texas at all times.

That ended the first convention of the Lone Star Party. The Party voted to have the next convention next year in Georgetown. It was as close to Austin as most Lone Star Party members dared to get. The board was also authorized to obtain a party headquarters building, preferably some dive on the east side of Austin near the French Legation.

Some delegates left at the close of the convention, others were going to have to drive much of the next day, so chose to stay over one more night. The Free Texas and Rampaging Elephants crews were philosophical at dinner.

"Just think of it, from the idea of Freedonia to referendum in about two years. Not a bad piece of work. We're moving in the right direction finally." the Rampaging Elephants host was pleased.

"Time to concentrate on the referendum and primary" said Ed.

"We may not have to worry about the primary too much. The Republican primary is going to get much more interesting. That will probably dictate where we need to run people and put most of the effort." suggested Roberts.

"Why not go for all of them?" asked Gene.

"Certainly for the scare factor. But we need enough seats to prevent the other two from having 76 so they have to form a coalition. We need at least 30 for that to happen. That is not as far away as some may think." was Ed's opinion

"I think it will pass, but the election combined with the primary means the Democrats are going to vote against it with more votes than would have opposed if it was not part of a candidate election. That puts an interesting wrinkle on it. Who is going to be motivated to show for the election?" said the owner of Rampaging Elephants.

"What about you Jim?" asked the host onn Rampaging Elephants.

Roberts said "I've got some militia business to take care of. We are either going to have to defend Texas from invasion, or assist in the people altering their government as they think fit."

There are times when it is enough to enjoy the company of friends and reflect on shared adventures. That was one of those times and they were pleased with the results to date of their labors. It made them even more motivated for the adventures to come. Either way the referendum went it was not yet over. As Churchill would say, it was not the beginning of the end, but it was the end of the beginning.

The next day, the last of the Lone Star Party delegates returned home. Much of the fun was over. Now the work started.

The Governor's Office called Gene Smith on Monday. The Governor was going to have a signing session for the referendum authorization, and the Lone Star Party was invited to send representatives to the signing as referendum supporters. Smith broke protocol by calling Roberts instead of notifying the executive board of the Lone Star Party.

"What do you think?" Smith asked.

Roberts answered "Interesting, I see the election politics of this thing has already started. The Lone Star Party supports the Governor. He'll be linking that to his campaign."

"Then we shouldn't go in your opinion?" queried Smith.

"Lone Star should be there. It gives you credibility as a player in the state." advised Roberts.

"Even if it benefits the Governor?" Smith continued the line of thought.

Roberts responded "I told you I hated politics, but Lone Star has to play. It comes with the territory. Remember that some in the movement wanted to form a political party years ago? This is what success brings."

"OK, thanks" Smith ended the conversation.

Smith then notified the executive board of the Governor's invitation. The Lone Star Party would be happy to attend and witness this important occasion.

At the signing ceremony, Lone Star was represented by Smith, McMasters, Greelow, and some of the other Free Texas County Directors that were on the executive board of the Lone Star Party. The Governor recognized the three attendees from their previous meeting. After conducting the signing ceremony, he spoke with the Lone Star representatives.

"Look who is back. This time you have a political party. I almost expected you not to be here. As I understand it, if not for your buddy Roberts at the convention, you wouldn't be here. Where is he?"

Gene Smith rose to the challenge. "He is back in Freedonia. Says he has important militia business that requires his attention. Something about defending Texas from invasion or a contingency in case politics fails. I think it was Mao who said that political power comes from the barrel of a gun."

The smile left the Governor's face. Well armed militias tend to have that effect on politicians. "I'll try to keep his efforts focused on the former, rather than the latter. It was nice to see you"

Most of the polls showed the referendum passing without too much difficulty. The pollsters were having some difficulty in getting good readings. It was hard to determine the support for the Lone Star Party and its impacts on the primary. In theory, the Lone Star party had the support of 30% to 40% of the Texas voters. When it got to specific candidates, the results were all over the place. It was entirely possible that there would be very few Lone Star primary races for the Lone Star voters to deal with. In such cases, the Lone Star supporters could go to the Republican primary and throw their weight behind a challenger to an incumbent and weaken him for the general election or even worse, defeat him. Such was the impact of the open primary system in Texas – voters are not registered to a political party until they vote in that party's primary. And they can change voting primary with no notice in the next election cycle. That helped to make Texas politics interesting.

The national news media were playing up the crazy Texans angle anytime the subject of politics in Texas came up. Attempts would be made to try to get Republican members of the Texas Congressional delegation to say something that might cost them support among the Lone Star Party voters. The left oriented internet space was having great fun with the referendum, too.

Some of the Lone Star supporters with a sense of humor started to have some fun with the leftists. They would go onto the blogs and social media and suggest that the country would be better off without Texas Tea Baggers, and Texas should be expelled from the United States. Competitions would be held to see who could get the highest number of liberals to agree to the idea of throwing Texas out of the United States.

Roberts thought it was a great idea. Keep repeating it often enough and liberals will take it up because it appeals to their sense of innate superiority over anyone not enlightened enough to be a progressive. They would never take a serious look at the consequences of forcing Texas out of the United States. They would be too overjoyed at the prospects of winning every Presidential election in the future and picking up House seats, to worry about losing the engine driving over 10% of the economic output of the United States.

To make sure that Texans were reminded of the contempt held for them by the national government in Washington, the Supreme Court scheduled the date for arguments in the case against Texas. Luckily for the left, the opinion from the Supreme Court would be made after referendum date. The coverage in the news would be sure to keep Texas informed and aware of the referendum.

Then the fear machine went to work. If Texas left the United States, all Social Security, Medicare, Veterans, and welfare payments would cease. Organizations could no longer get their government grants. School children would go hungry. Banks would have to cancel your credit card. The list of sky is falling items seemed endless. One of the Free Texas supporters remarked, they forgot the one about if Texas leaves the United States, the ice cream in my freezer will melt.

As the referendum date got closer, polls consistently showed support at just over 50%. Passage or failure would depend on who showed up to vote. That was always the case when it got close. The vote to admit Texas into the United States made it through Congress because of a changed vote by Senator Henry Johnson of Louisiana.

Most of the Lone Star Party supporters came to the conclusion that the referendum needed to pass. A failure would set back the ability for Texas to turn back the growth in federal power. Somebody needed to stand up to the Leviathan, and that somebody was Texas. Free Texas and Lone Star supporters started to organize watch parties to see the results after the polls closed. Many of the supporters would be working at the polls to gain experience in serving as poll watchers and election judges. Lone Star had taken Joseph Stalin's admonition to heart – to vote is nothing, to count the votes is everything.

Finally, election Tuesday arrived, and Texans headed for the polls. Reports were that turnout was slightly higher than for previous primary elections. Only in some of the larger cities did Lone Star have contested primaries. For the most part, Lone Star candidates could concentrate on the general election in November. The Republican primary would be the interesting news in the minds of the Lone Star supporters. How many incumbents might get taken out in the primary was the question. It would be a major coup if the Speaker of the House lost to a challenger.

Borden County returns were counted 30 minutes after the polls closed. The referendum passed with some 90% of the vote. In the big picture, that was meaningless. Borden County was where the referendum was likely to do the best in the state. The Freedonia town square became the watch party, as results came in. The rural counties were generally the first to report as there are so few ballots to count. The referendum was winning easily with 70% or more of the vote. Totals from the urban counties were slow to come in. The deciding factor would be how the Republican voters felt about the referendum. Were they going to take it seriously, or as a joke and not bother.

The referendum was doing fine in the medium size counties as the results started to be reported. It was passing by a 2 to 1 margin. Next to report are the heavily Republican suburbs. The winning percentage was still over 60% in those counties. Now, some meaningful totals were being reported from larger cities. The referendum was losing in Travis County 2 to 1. That was no surprise from the Peoples Republic of Austin.

Statewide totals were starting to tally with meaningful numbers. The FOR margin was still in the 60s, but dropping throughout the evening. By 10 PM, the margin had fallen below 60%. The drop continued toward 11 PM, and then reporting percentages started to hit 95% to 97%. There were not that many more votes to count. The referendum was called a pass with 54% of the vote.

There was relief around the town square of Freedonia.

"Jim, looks like you might make it to Switzerland to ski yet." Ed McMasters teased.

Jim Roberts would never ski again.

Epilogue

It is my sincere wish that you found this work worth the investment of your time and treasure. Should this book prove popular, it would be the first book of a trilogy. The next book would take these characters through Texas independence and the possible breakup of the United Stares due the political stress that can not be resolved to the satisfaction of all the factions which now compose the population of the country. The third book would be the results of Texas independence on Texas and the world.